DESKTOP PUBLISHING

MEDIA WORKSHOP

DESKTOP PUBLISHING

The Art of Communication

John Madama

LERNER PUBLICATIONS COMPANY
MINNEAPOLIS

To Taylor, whose curiosity, laughter, and love of learning recreate the world.

Library of Congress Cataloging-in-Publication Data

Madama, John
Desktop publishing : the art of communication / John Madama.
p. cm.—(Media workshop)
Includes index.
Summary: Explains the desktop publishing process including computer basics, necessary writing and research skills, working with illustrations and photographs, typography, design, layout, production, and printing.
ISBN 0-8225-2303-5 (library binding)
1. Desktop publishing—Juvenile literature. [1. Desktop publishing.]
I. Title. II. Series: Media workshop (Series)
Z286.D47M343 1993
686.2'254416—dc20 91-46314
CIP
AC

Manufactured in the United States of America

1 2 3 4 5 6 98 97 96 95 94 93

Contents

17 items 1,077K in disk 339K available

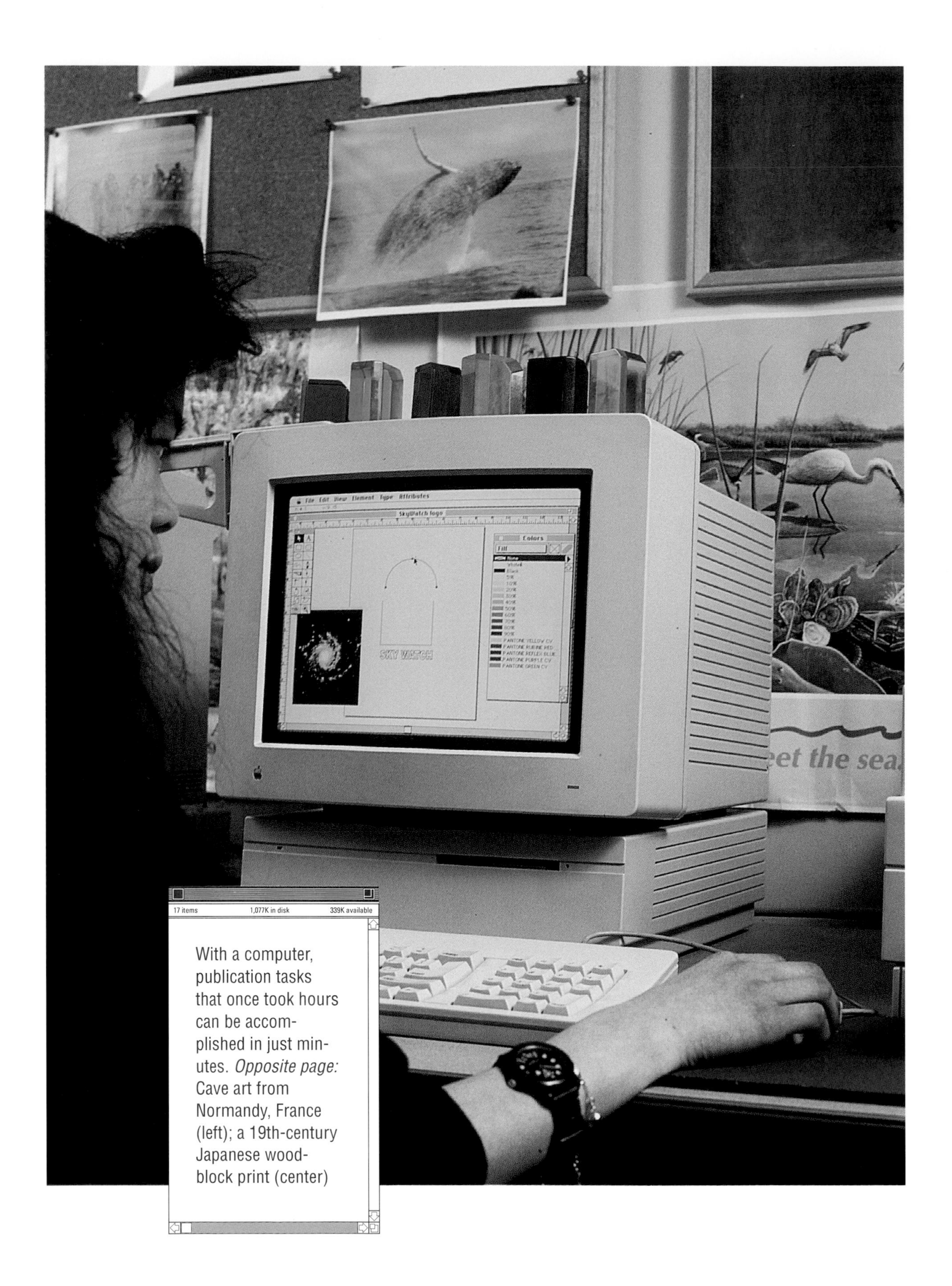

With a computer, publication tasks that once took hours can be accomplished in just minutes. *Opposite page:* Cave art from Normandy, France (left); a 19th-century Japanese woodblock print (center)

Chapter One

The Communication Revolution

Thirty thousand years ago, humans created the first graphic forms of communication by painting and drawing on the walls of caves. These simple yet powerful images of animals and people are the earliest records of human thought, needs, and dreams. The early artists used sticks, the edges of rocks, charcoal, and pigments from soil to scrape or draw their pictures. These images came to be known as "pictographs."

Over thousands of years, pictographs evolved into the letters of alphabets. Written language enabled ancient peoples, including the Greeks and Romans, to record and store large amounts of information and communicate complex ideas. In ancient times, few people had access to written information. Public libraries and bookstores did not exist, and only a small fraction of the population knew how to read. Writing was an art practiced by specialists called scribes. The only way to reproduce a document was to have a scribe copy it by hand.

Printing, the mass reproduction of artwork and written materials, was invented in Asia during the 9th century. The early Asian method of printing was called wood-block printing. For each page, images were carved into a block of wood. The woodcut was then covered with ink and pressed repeatedly onto sheets of paper.

In about A.D.1450, a German named Johannes Gutenberg invented a method of quickly reproducing documents using a hand-operated printing press. Gutenberg's press contained letters that could be moved and arranged to spell any word. Printing with movable type was faster and less expensive than wood-block printing. Whereas wood-blocks were carved for use in one publication, movable letters could be used again and again.

Movable type revolutionized the distribution of information to the public. Books, maps, and newspapers became affordable and widespread. More people learned to read. Publishing, the art and business of creating and distributing printed information, became an engine for change and innovation in society.

A medieval printing press

The hand-operated printing press was replaced in 1814 by the first steam-powered press. The first mechanical **typesetting** machine, which could set an entire line of type at once, was invented in the 1880s. Other inventions that improved the speed and quality of publishing soon followed. These devices included the camera and photographic film, typewriters, and modern presses capable of running 100,000 printed sheets per hour!

The Computer Revolution

Computer technology has started another revolution in communication. Computers are electronic devices that can store, retrieve, and process information. The first computers, invented in the United States during the 1950s, were used to analyze large amounts of data (information) and perform complex mathematical equations. These early machines were large and expensive and were only available to big corporations and universities.

It was not until the 1980s that personal microcomputers ("micro" means small) became commonplace in homes, schools, and small businesses. Personal computers are portable and affordable. They allow you to store vast amounts of information and retrieve it within seconds. You can solve equations, write papers, draw pictures, create graphs, and even play games on your personal computer. Computers are fun to use. They encourage you to experiment and be creative, and they strengthen your analytical skills.

Desktop publishing is the art of using a computer to combine words and images into an attractive publication. A computer publishing system can help you create newsletters, posters, and brochures. Before the invention of the computer, publishing required a roomful of expensive equipment and many specialists. With computer technology, one person can operate a publishing system that fits on a desk. Computers make publishing easier, faster, and less costly.

This book will show desktop publishers how to design and print great-looking publications that will attract readers and hold their attention. This book will not teach you how to use a specific brand of equipment or a specific computer program. Instead, you will learn about writing, **typography**, illustration, and layout techniques important to all desktop publishers. You will also find a chapter on the equipment you will need to set up your own desktop publishing system.

Although the desktop publisher uses

modern electronic devices to communicate, the creative process remains the same as it was for the earliest publishers. Desktop publishers communicate with words and images, experiment, and use knowledge from the past to build the future.

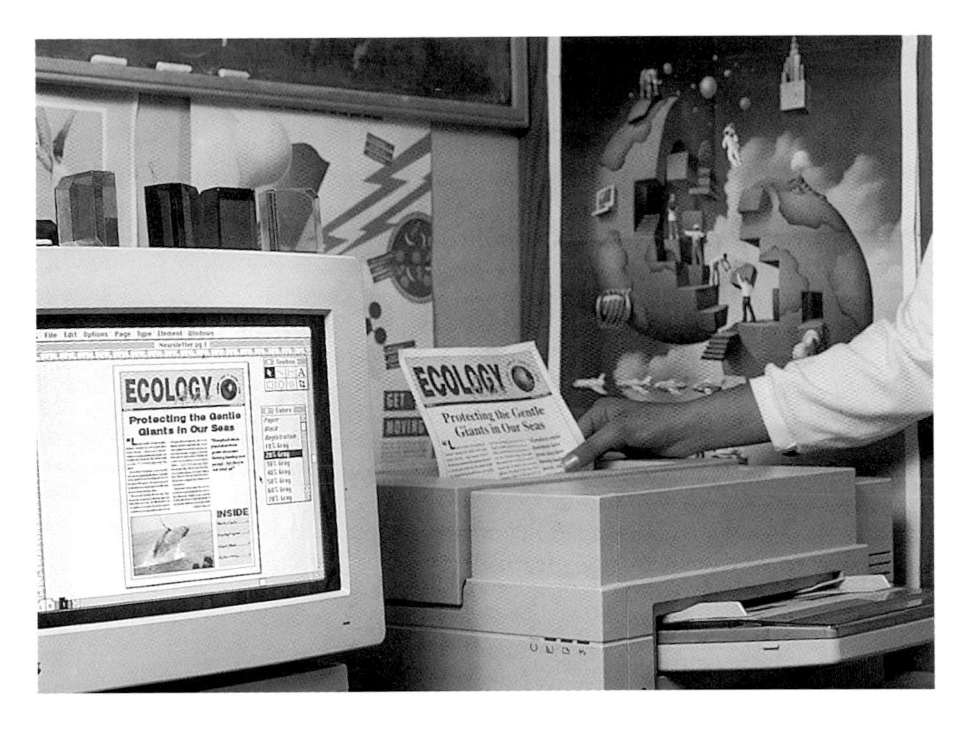

With a desktop publishing system, layout pages come out of a printer complete and ready for reproduction.

Before Desktop Publishing

17 items | 1,077K in disk | 339K available

Without a desktop publishing system, the publication process can be complex and expensive. Text is sent to an outside company to be typeset. Artwork is reduced, enlarged, and prepared for printing using a costly photostat camera. A specialist called a keyliner (right) pastes the type and artwork onto a layout board using wax or rubber cement. With a T square and ruler, the keyliner makes sure that headlines, captions, text, and artwork are properly aligned and that spacing is consistent throughout the publication.

Traditional layout designs are difficult to change. Type or artwork that has been pasted into a layout must be pulled up, remeasured, and repositioned by hand. When designing with the computer, however, repositioning and resizing is done electronically—within seconds.

A microcomputer is portable and affordable. Most schools and businesses, and many individuals, own personal computers. *Opposite page:* A mouse

Chapter Two

HARDWARE AND SOFTWARE

The elegance of a computer system is its simplicity. Once inside a computer, all words and images are converted into strings of simple "on" or "off" electronic signals. The "on" signal is represented by the digital number one (1). "Off" is represented by the digit zero (0). Every letter of the alphabet has a different on/off code. The letter **A**, for instance, consists of eight on and off signals written as 01000001. When we talk about a series of digits carried by a computer, we are referring to **digital information.**

The digital information in a computer system flows though miniature electronic circuits and mechanical devices that store, display, and print words and images. The mechanical equipment in a computer system is called **hardware.** Computers have hardware devices for inputting, processing, displaying, storing, and outputting

(printing) information. **Software** refers to the programs, or instructions, that tell the computer hardware what to do. Software lets you use the computer to perform specific tasks, such as word processing or drawing.

Input

One of the most important devices for inputting, or entering, digital information into a computer is a **keyboard.** A keyboard allows you to type words, numbers, and symbols into your computer and to edit information on the computer monitor, or screen. Many computers come with a **mouse**, a small movable tool that you use like a pointer. A mouse allows you to select, move, draw, and edit information and images on the computer screen.

Another important tool for inputting

information is a **scanner**. Scanners convert graphic images, such as photographs, into digital information that can be read by a computer.

All computers have a **disk drive.** The disk drive reads digital information and instructions from computer software and can send the information to the monitor and to the computer's **central processing unit.**

Processing

The central processing unit (CPU) is the brain of the computer. The CPU consists of thousands of microscopic electrical circuits mounted on small silicon chips. A CPU is rated by the amount of digital information that it can hold and the speed at which it can process information (perform mathematical calculations or draw pictures, for instance). A personal computer can instantly process about 400 pages of text. The amount of information a computer can process at one time is called its **memory.**

Display

Digital information entered into a computer can be displayed on a video monitor. Once on the display, text or graphics can be edited or altered using a keyboard and a mouse.

The video monitor contains a grid of small squares called **pixels.** Each individual pixel can be turned on (lit up) or left off. When a series of pixels are lit up, the pixels create a **bit map,** showing words or images on the screen.

There are three types of video monitors: monochromatic (one color), grayscale, and color. Low-cost monochromatic monitors can display pixels in one color only, such as white, green, or amber. Grayscale monitors can display up to 256 shades of gray and thus can show a photograph as a realistic image on the computer screen. Color monitors provide the most versatile screen display. The least expensive color monitors can display 16 different colors. The best color monitors can display millions of colors.

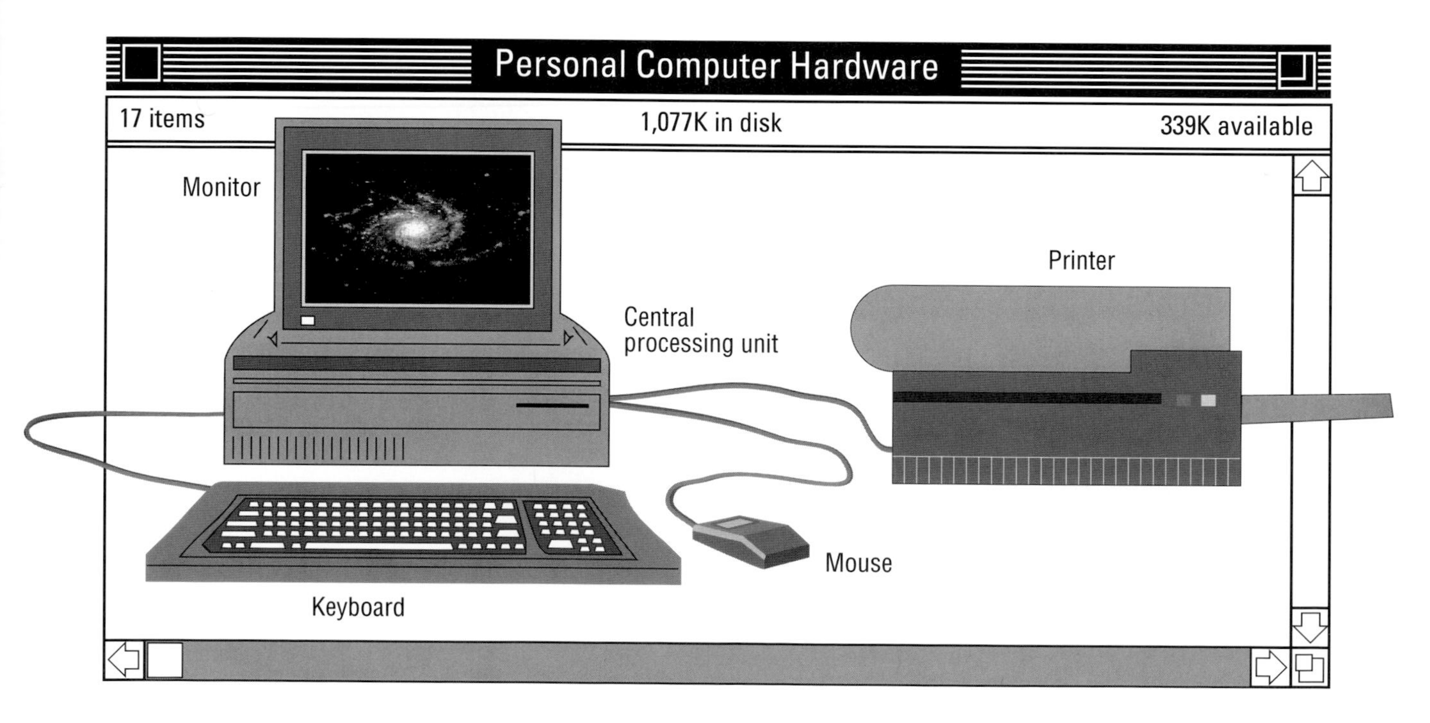

By magnifying this computer screen image 200, 400, and 800 percent, we can see how a series of pixels creates a picture.

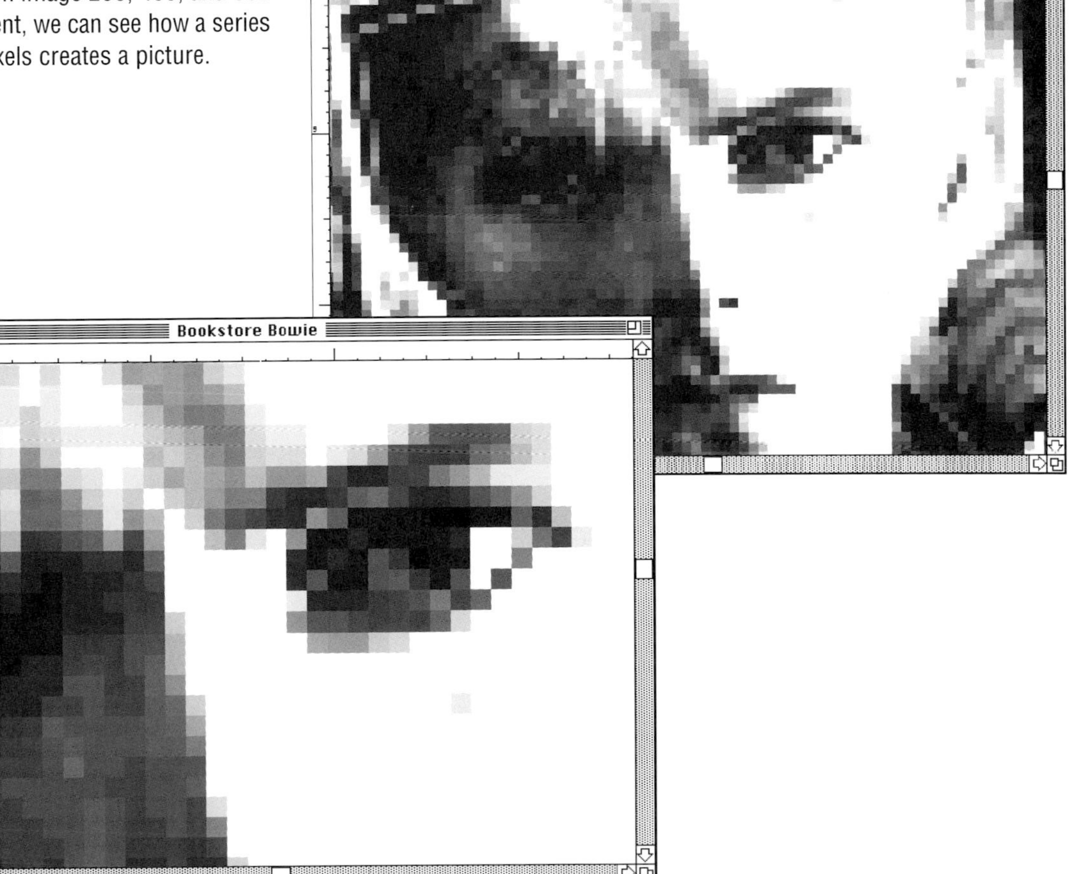

Purchasing Your Desktop System

15 items | 1,370K in disk | 46K available

The units of digital information that a computer processes and stores are called *bytes*. One byte equals a single alphabet character such as the letter A. All computers and disks are rated by how many bytes they can process and store.

The letter K (for kilo) is used to describe 1,000 bytes of information. One page of type equals about 2K, or 2,000 bytes. A standard, double-sided floppy storage disk holds 800K, which equals about 400 pages of text.

When purchasing a desktop publishing system, you'll want a computer that can process at least 1 million bytes (called 1 megabyte or 1 meg) of information and can store 20 million bytes (20 megs) on a hard disk. One million bytes is equal to about 500 pages of text.

If you will be using a scanner to input photos, you will want to buy a computer with at least 2 megs of processing ability and a 40-meg hard disk for storage.

Storage

Digital information is stored on special hardware components called disks. **Hard disks** are rigid metal platters that make a magnetic recording of computer data. A small hard disk can store more than 10,000 pages of text.

Floppy disks are made of plastic and Mylar film. Floppy disks are portable storage units that can be inserted into and removed from a computer. They are used to transfer data from one computer to another, to load software programs onto a hard disk, and to store data.

When you enter information into a computer, you should store your work on both a floppy disk and the computer's hard disk. This duplication of storage is called "making a backup." If one disk is damaged, your data will be preserved on the backup.

Inserting a floppy disk into a disk drive

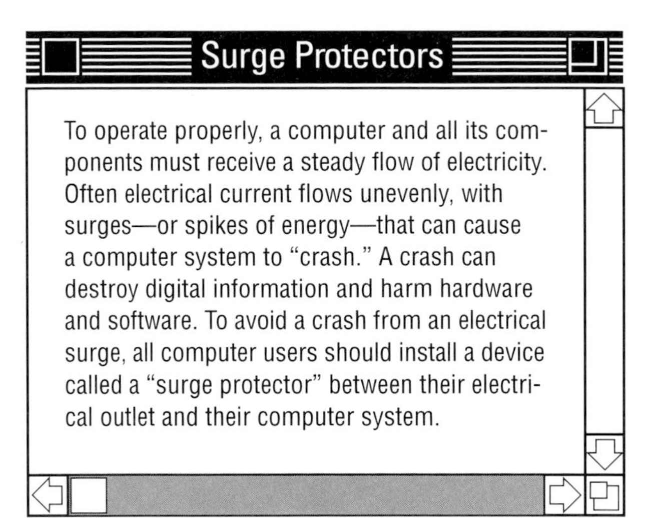

Surge Protectors

To operate properly, a computer and all its components must receive a steady flow of electricity. Often electrical current flows unevenly, with surges—or spikes of energy—that can cause a computer system to "crash." A crash can destroy digital information and harm hardware and software. To avoid a crash from an electrical surge, all computer users should install a device called a "surge protector" between their electrical outlet and their computer system.

Output

Text and images can be outputted, or printed, on one of several types of printers. The quality of a printer is judged on the **resolution**, or sharpness, of the text or image it prints. Resolution is measured by the term *dpi*, which stands for "dots per inch." The greater the dot-per-inch output of a printer the better the quality of the image.

The most basic printers, called dot matrix printers, have resolution values of 144 dpi. In one square inch, a 144-dpi printer can lay down 20,736 (144 x 144) dots. Generally, the images produced by dot matrix printers are not sharp enough for quality desktop publishing.

Laser printers use a high-energy beam of light to print 300 dpi. In one square inch, a 300-dpi printer can produce 90,000 (300 x 300) dots. Laser printers are suitable for printing art and type for many kinds of desktop publications.

The highest resolution printers are called "imagesetters." Imagesetters have resolutions of 1,200 dpi (more than 1.4 million dots per square inch), 2,500 dpi (more than 6 million dots per square inch), or more. Imagesetters are very expensive and are used

Images outputted with a dot-matrix printer (1), a laser printer (2), and an imagesetter (3)

by professional publishers who work with detailed graphics and photographs. Desktop publishers who have a basic computer system can, for a fee, have their files printed on an imagesetter at a service bureau—a professional graphics or printing business.

Software

"Software" refers to sets of instructions that operate computer hardware and that let you do specific jobs on the computer, such as drawing or page layout. Another name for a piece of software is a "program." The two most important kinds of software are operating system software and application software.

Operating system software runs all the hardware components in your computer system, including the monitor, the hard disk, and the printer. Operating system software is specific to each computer brand. That is, IBM system software works only with IBM-compatible computers. Computer companies update their system software regularly. If you register your computer when you buy it, the company will notify you when upgraded operating system software is available.

Application software lets you perform specific tasks with your computer, such as writing, data processing, and graphing. Let's look at the most important application software programs for the desktop publisher.

Word processing software allows you to type and edit lists, reports, and articles on a computer. Word processing software can create different sizes and styles of type, set margins, number pages, count words, alphabetize lists, and more. Most word processing programs contain a dictionary to help you check spelling and properly hyphenate, or divide, words at the end of a line.

Drawing programs let you create geometric shapes on the computer that can be filled with shades and patterns. You can combine shapes to make pictures, logos, and diagrams. Most graphic elements found in major newspapers are created with computer drawing programs.

Painting programs contain electronic tools that act like paintbrushes and erasers. Paintbrush tools are used to create images that have a painted or textured appearance. Eraser tools are used to remove unwanted portions of pictures.

Many software companies sell disks containing "clip art," finished artwork—created in drawing or painting programs by professional artists—that desktop users can include in their own publications.

Image processing, or scanning, software allows a desktop publisher to scan, alter, and apply special effects to artwork and photographs. In many ways, owning image processing software is like having a photography lab in your computer.

Page layout software allows you to combine type, drawings, and images into a layout or design. Page layout programs let you create documents as small as business cards or as large as posters. Once you establish the size and shape of your layout, files can be **imported**, or transferred, from word processing, painting, or drawing programs and arranged in a design in your page layout program. You can also draw images and type words with page layout software.

An “Ecology Action” reporter interviews a whale watch guide for a story on hump-back whales. *Opposite page:* One person can operate a desktop system, but by working as team, each person can focus on his or her specialty.

Chapter Three

The Publishing Team

The desktop publisher's goal is to create an attractive publication composed of words and pictures. To reach this goal, you might find it helpful to break the publication process into a series of steps. The entire process can be carried out by one person or by a team.

Let's follow the production of an ecology newsletter published by a group of students and their teacher. Each person is responsible for certain tasks. The major assignments are writing, editing, photography, illustration, and design.

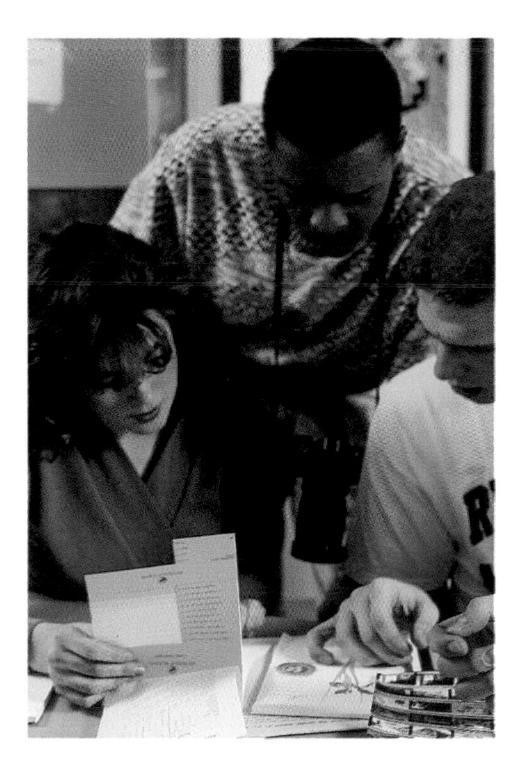

The *writer* researches and writes informational articles and works closely with the editor to produce the final draft of each story. Writers use word processing software.

The *editor* reviews the first draft of each story or article and looks for errors in spelling and grammar. He or she also checks the story for accuracy and logical organization. Finally, the editor meets with the writer and offers suggestions for ways to improve each story.

The *photographer* takes or locates photographs of people, places, or events mentioned in the writer's articles. The photographer uses image processing software and works closely with the illustrator and designer.

The *illustrator* creates images that support and enhance each story. He or she uses drawing, painting, and image processing (scanning) software and works closely with the photographer and designer.

The *designer* creates a layout that will combine the text and artwork provided by the other team members. The designer gives assignments to the photographer and illustrator and makes arrangements to have the publication reproduced at a commercial printing or copy shop. Designers use page layout software.

Planning Your Publication

Although team members work independently, they must also meet as a group to make editorial decisions. The ecology newsletter staff first meets to determine the purpose and the audience for the newsletter. The meeting will help determine the writing style and format of the publication. An ecology newsletter, a business report, a promotion for a rock concert, and a brochure for a health club will each have a unique look and style.

After a brainstorming and discussion session, the newsletter team came up with the following statement of purpose:

> Our goal is to publish (three times a year) a four-page environmental newsletter that is action-oriented and that will inform students, teachers, and parents about local conservation issues, endangered animal species, and ecology club activities.

With this purpose and audience in mind, the team meets again to discuss story content, set deadlines, choose a system for managing computer files, and write up a budget for their newsletter.

The students decide that each newsletter issue will contain two major stories: one on an endangered species and one on a conservation issue. One section will be devoted to activities readers can do to help the environment.

For the first newsletter, the students decide to feature an article about their town's new recycling program and a story about whales. Future newsletters will include articles about wolves, owls, energy conservation, and wetlands.

Deadlines are an important part of the publishing process because they establish a fixed production schedule. Deadlines make each individual responsible for keeping the production process moving and seeing that the publication is printed on time. If someone misses a deadline, all other deadlines might have to be pushed back. The team must set due dates for first drafts, final drafts, layout designs, artwork, and printing. Set reasonable deadlines and stick to them.

Be sure to label each floppy disk and make backup copies of every file.

Since most of the ecology newsletter text, artwork, and layouts will be inputted or created on a computer, the group must set up a system for managing their computer files. Computer files can be organized just like office files. For instance, the ecology team sets up a "folder," or file, on their computer's hard disk for each issue of the newsletter. Each folder contains smaller files for text, artwork, and layouts. Team members always make floppy disk backups of their files.

The budget is a plan showing how much money it will cost to produce, print, and distribute a publication. The ecology news-letter team has a limited amount of money to spend. They create a budget to determine how many pages they will have in their newsletter, how many copies they can print, whether they can print in more than one color, and how much money they can spend on computer disks, film, photo processing, and mailing.

Chapter Four

Creative Story Writing

Stories are the foundation of a publication. A good story will inform, entertain, motivate, or instruct your readers. To capture a reader's attention, make your characters and topics come alive. As the great writer Mark Twain explained, "Don't say the old lady screamed—bring her on and let her scream."

Story writing begins with a review of the purpose and audience for your publication. Ask youself, "What do I want to say and who will be listening?" Good journalism skills are built by practice, persistence, and by understanding some guidelines for effective written communication.

The Writing Process

A well-written story begins with thorough research. Go to the library to locate books or magazine articles about your subject. Avoid using information that is more than ten years old—especially when researching a scientific topic. Take notes and write down the names of titles and authors. When you write your own article, make sure to credit your sources properly.

Interview experts in the field of ecology, recycling, or whatever topic you choose to write on. Prepare a set of questions ahead of time. Get the experts talking about their work. Make sure you spell their names correctly and quote them accurately. Quotes give authority to your story. If possible, tape record the interview. Observe and describe your surroundings. Give the reader a sense of place and mood.

Organize your notes into an outline. Stories are divided into three principal parts: lead, body, and ending. The lead (or introduction) draws the reader into the topic. The body provides facts, statistics, and quotes. The ending, or conclusion, summarizes the story and provides a base for further thought or a plea for action.

Putting the first words on paper or into the computer is often the hardest part of the writing process. The best writers in the world stall and go through false starts before the right words come out. Don't become discouraged. A perfect story is rarely created with the first draft. Your words will go through several editing and review stages before becoming a polished, inviting story. Here are a few tips to improve your writing skills:

• Know how many words you need to write for your story. For the ecology newsletter, each story will contain between 500 and 700 words (about two typed pages). Most word processing software can keep a running tally of the number of words in a document.

• Be concise and direct. Use short, simple sentences constructed mainly of nouns and verbs. Action verbs are engines that drive your story. Avoid using too many adverbs and adjectives. Don't use a long or unfamiliar word if a short, simple word carries the

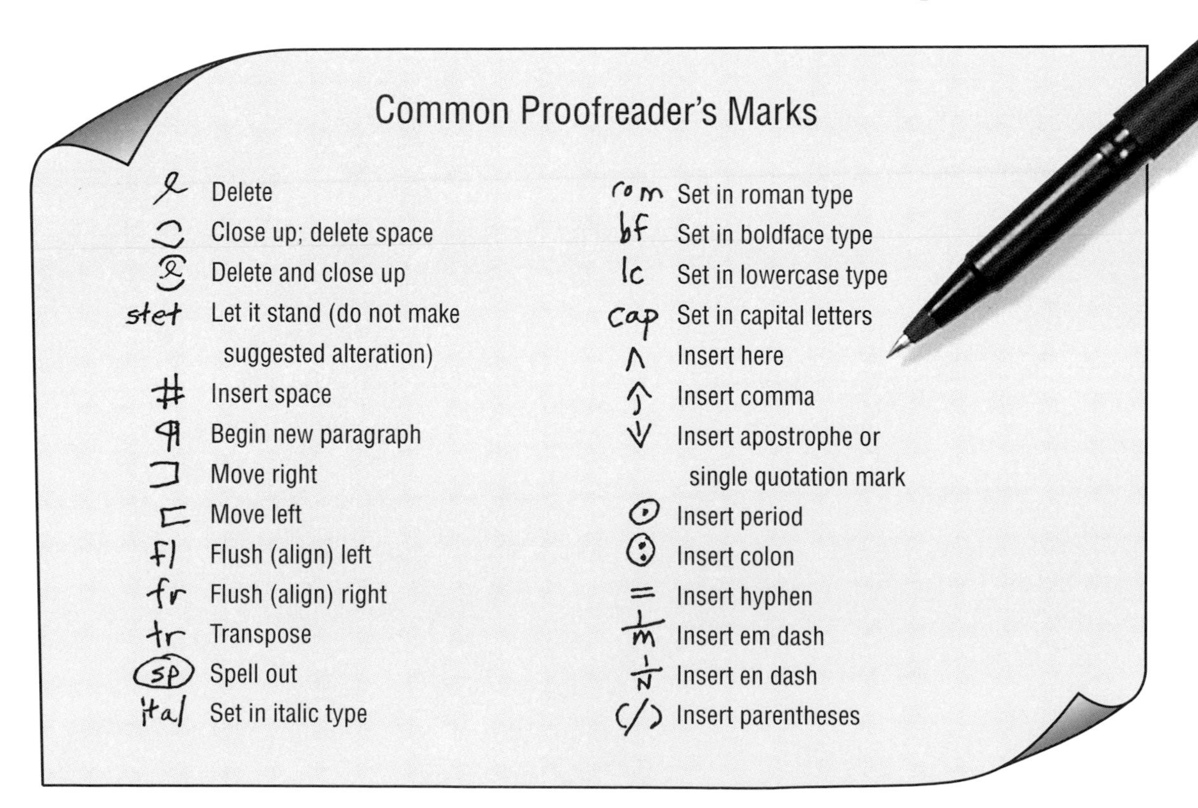

Whales and Dolphins:
Six Things You Can Do

- Support the protection of coastal wetlands. Coastal wetlands produce food for life in the ocean. Currents carry this food to areas where whale live and feed.
- Write letters to seafood companies to find alternative fishing techniques that don't trap dolphins with commercial fish.
- Recycle! Recycling waste reduces pollution from dumps that leak into water supplies and eventually flow to the ocean.
- Don't use pesticides and chemicals for lawns and gardens. Pesticides are poison fro all forms of life. There are many organic alternatives for growing healthy greenspaces.
- Support environmental research and education by joining and actively working with local and U.S. ecology organizations.
- Write letters to local, state and national government officials to suppport the highest level of sewage treatment and the cleanup of urban harbors.

The editor makes sure each article is easy to understand and free of errors in grammar and spelling.

The "Ecology Action" writers ask a teacher to review a draft of each article.

same meaning. Shorten a sentence if possible.

• Avoid using "be verbs" such as *was, has been,* and *would be.* "Be verbs" create a passive voice and make your sentences weak and wordy. For example, "The sky was darkened by clouds" is more powerful when changed to: "Clouds darkened the sky."

• Keep paragraphs short, especially in journalistic writing. Look at a newspaper—most paragraphs are no more than two or three sentences long.

• Vary the number of words in different sentences to give your story an interesting pace or rhythm. An article with sentences that are mostly the same length will have a monotonous tone. Read the story aloud. Your ear will tell you how the pace sounds and if the words flow rhythmically.

• Have a friend read each story and critique it. Don't be afraid of criticism. Use input from others to build a better story.

• Use a dictionary, a thesaurus, and a grammar book when needed.

Word Processing Tips

• Print the first draft of your story as double-spaced text. Double-spacing gives the editor room between lines to write suggestions and changes.

• Place only one space after a period instead of two. The sharp, clean type from a laser printer or imagesetter looks best with one space between sentences.

• Use word processing software that has a "spell checker," or dictionary, containing at least 80,000 words. Don't depend completely on the dictionary, however. Always read through a hard copy (a printed draft) of your story and check for errors. Spell checkers cannot tell if you meant "write" when you typed "right" or if you meant "principal" and typed "principle." Most software allows you to create a "user dictionary" of special terms and names you use often. Some word processing software contains an "electronic thesaurus" that will help you find alternatives to frequently used words.

• Name your stories and save them in the proper file on your hard disk. Always make a backup copy of your files.

• Print out several draft copies of each story—one for each member of the newsletter team. The designer, photographer, and illustrator can review your first draft and begin to think about art and photographs that will enhance each story.

Good writing skills are developed by practice, patience, and attention to detail.

Editorial Review and Markup

The editor reviews the first draft of each story for errors in spelling, fact, grammar, and style. Editors make sure that the writing style is appropriate for the publication's intended audience and that ideas and paragraphs flow logically.

The editor and writer work together to produce the final draft of each article. They review the stories and discuss changes.They choose headlines and decide if the stories need subheadings that will help organize the information more clearly. The final draft of each story will be given to the designer.

The design process involves placing type and graphics into an attractive, balanced page layout. *Opposite page:* Photographs are an important part of a newsletter.

Chapter Five

The Design Process

The design is the visual plan for your publication. The design process involves placing stories and artwork together into an attractive, well-balanced layout. The design should be easy on the eye and should help the audience understand and remember the stories. A dynamic design will pull readers into the page and hold their attention.

Look at other publications to stimulate ideas for your own newsletter design. For an ecology newsletter, you might visit a local nature center or review publications from national environmental organizations. Notice how other designers and illustrators use graphic techniques. Make copies of designs that you find attractive.

Review each story and look for passages to be used as "callouts"—important sentences or quotations, set in large type—which will give the reader a preview of the story. Think of pictures that would help explain the story or bring it to life. Mark sentences that require illustration and mark statistics that could be turned into a helpful chart or graph.

Finding Illustrations

Will you take photographs yourself or draw illustrations? Do you know of organizations that might give you free photographs? Will you need permission to copy images from other publications?

Write down names, addresses, and phone numbers of people and organizations to contact. Make sure to give them credit if you use their illustrations in the finished newsletter. Make a list of the artwork needed for each story and give photography and illustration assignments to the appropriate person on your newsletter team.

Planning the Page Format

Next, determine the page format, or "page specifications," for your newsletter. How large will your publication be? How many pages will it have? Will your newsletter have a vertical (tall) or horizontal (wide) shape? How wide will the margins be? How many columns will you use per page? Page layout software enables you to automatically create a page format to suit your needs.

Some common page sizes are standard letter (8½-by-11 inches), legal (8½-by-14), tabloid (11-by-17), and poster (14-by-17).

Using your page format as a guide, draw pencil sketches (called "thumbnails") showing how text and artwork might appear on each page. Experiment with different designs. Your final sketch will serve as your guide when you are ready to lay out the publication on the computer screen.

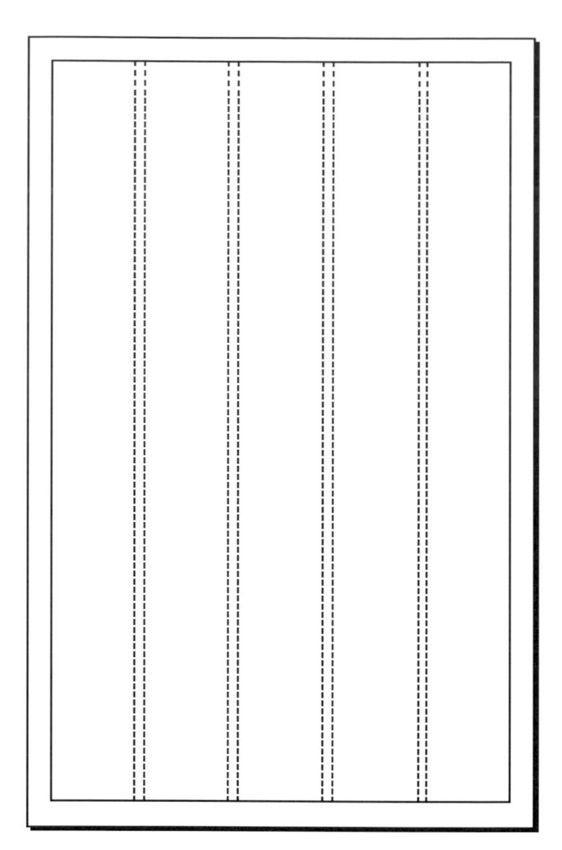

Tabloid size (11 x 17)
Five columns

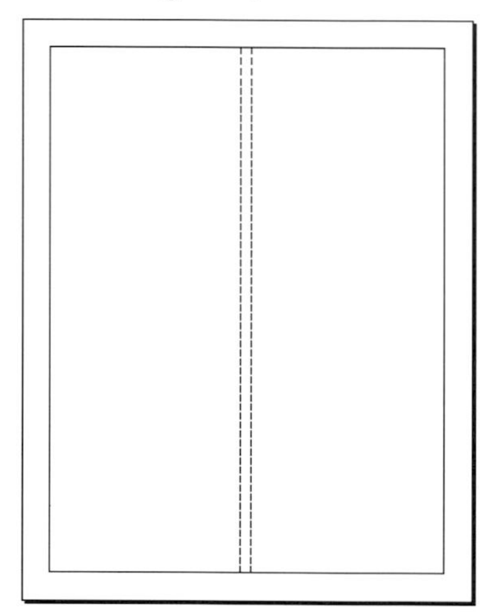

Letter size (8 1/2 x 11)
Two columns

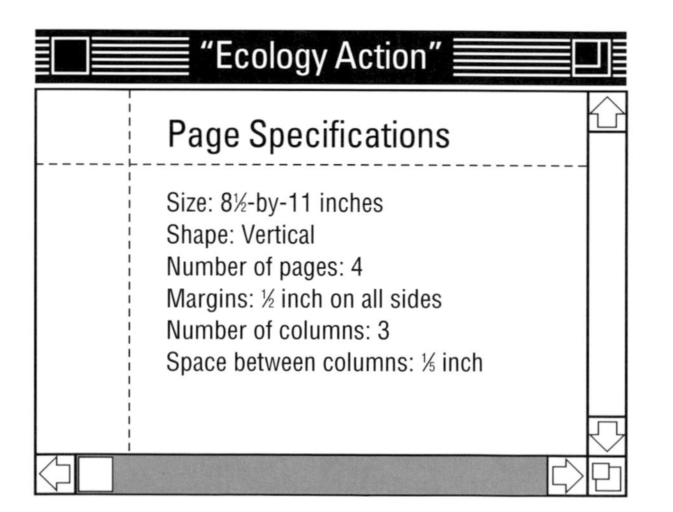

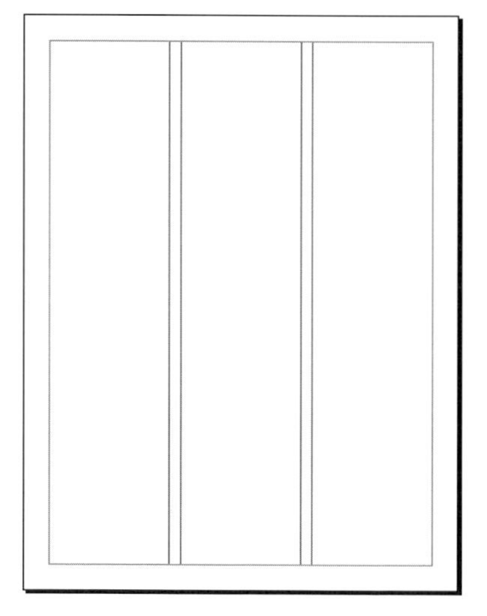

Letter size (8½ x 11)
Three columns

Six Goals of Effective Communication

15 items 1,370K in disk 46K available

Readable text
Well-written and accurate text is essential for conveying information. Edit your text for correct spelling and grammar. Choose a typeface that is easy to read. Add sufficient space between lines of type so that the type "breathes." Use italic and bold type to create contrast or highlight information.

Simple, balanced layout
Organize text and graphics without crowding information. Let the page breathe. Use white space to relieve and prevent eye strain. Create a layout that moves the reader's eye around the page. Note in the example how the layout takes a pyramid shape, using a single headline block, two pictures, and three columns of text.

Attractive, inviting images
Use photographs that are in focus and related to your story. Use line art illustrations to support and enhance the text. Note how the African woman in the photo is looking into the page and down toward the type and zebra graphic. This image leads the reader's eye into the story.

Illustrated concepts
Graphics are most effective when they help the reader understand the text. Illustrate statistics with charts and graphs. Drawings help the reader better understand scientific concepts.

Consistency of graphic style
Be consistent when sizing and spacing text, headlines, and subheads. Mixed styles and sizes will confuse a reader. Lines, boxes, and shadows should be of similar weight and tone.

A fresh approach
Be bold. Experiment to create a unique layout or graphic. The computer is a great tool because it allows you to make changes in a design and instantly print the results.

AFRICA

The Roots of Civilization

Masai

The grasslands of Africa support one of the most unique collections of animals in the world. At anywhere along this part your tour you may see an 18 foot giraffe nibbling at a mimosa tree; impalas and gazelles bounding across a plain or hear the earth-shaking roar of a 500 pound lion. Alongside the animals of this land live over 100 human societies. We will take a 3 day climb of the snow-capped Mt. Kilimangaro and visit the Masai tribe.

Bushmen

The Kalahari Desert of Southern Africa is a dry, harsh environment that supports the nomadic life of the Bushmen tribe. Bushmen hunt antelopes with poison arrows and gather ostrich eggs and wild nuts to survive. We'll visit an ancient Bushmen Rock Art site and hear folktales about the the animal/human "god" Kraggen. Travel in the desert will be in 4-wheel drive Land Rovers so we can visit a beautiful remote palm oasis.

Pygmies

The jungle home of the Pygmies lies deep in a thick tangle of plants in the shadow of a towering mountain range called the Baba Tiba - The Mountains of the Moon. The forest community contains thousands of exotic animals, birds and insects including monkeys, anteaters, crocodiles, hippos, and elephants. The Rain Forest tour will include a visit to a pygmy campsite and participation in the construction of mangongo tree hut.

Desktop publishers can chose from hundreds of different typefaces. *Opposite page:* Measuring type with a type gauge

Chapter Six

TYPE: THE ARCHITECTURE OF LANGUAGE

One of the designer's most important responsibilities is choosing type for a publication. With the art of typography, a desktop publisher helps readers better understand written material. Typography transforms plain typewritten text into attractive letterforms—making the text easier to read and more inviting. The proper type can help express a feeling, attract attention, or convey a message. Designers often say that type has "personality."

After the writers and editors have submitted their final articles for publication, the designer must "format" the text. Basic type formatting, usually done with word processing software, involves choosing a **typeface**, selecting a type size and style, and determining the spacing between lines. Advanced type formatting, done with page layout software, gives you precise control over the spacing between letters and words and allows you to create special effects with type.

Type formatting helps a desktop publisher to effectively communicate the writer's message. Well-formatted type appears even and rhythmic. The spacing between individual letters and words is balanced.

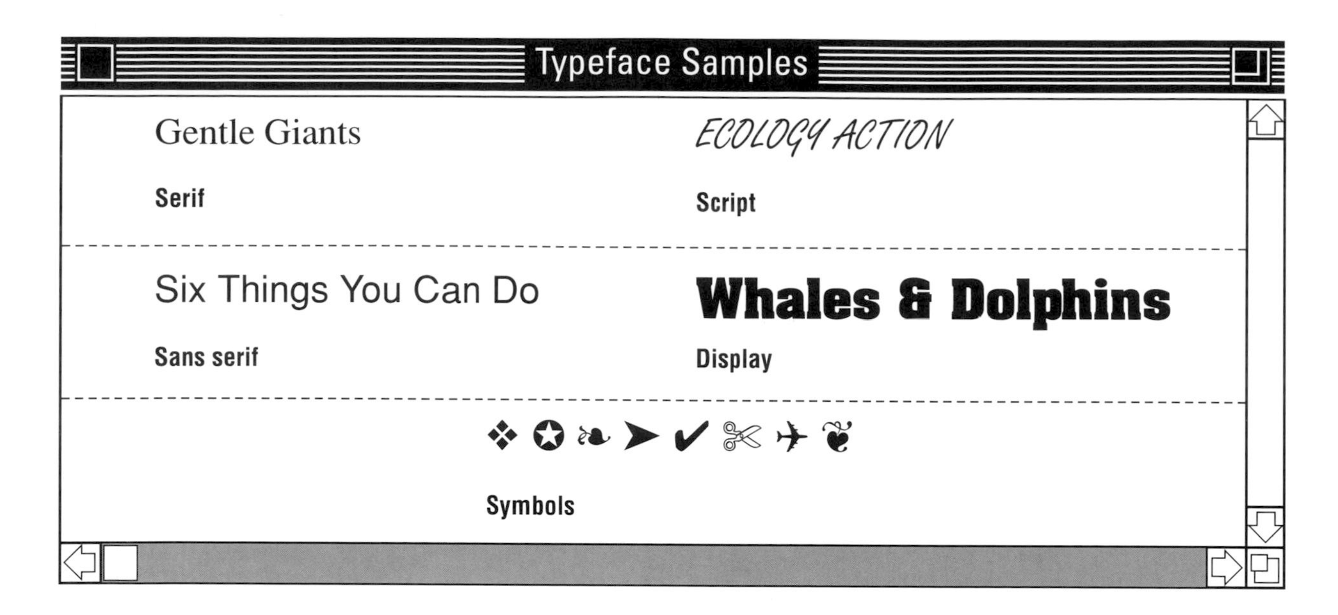

Typefaces

Designers are responsible for choosing appropriate and readable typefaces for headlines, subheads, and body copy. Often, publishers use one typeface for text and another for headlines. Although there are hundreds of typefaces, professional publishers usually use no more than three faces per publication. Too many typefaces can make a publication look unfocused or send a confusing message.

Typefaces are grouped into five main categories: serif, sans serif, display, script, and symbols.

Serif typefaces have serifs, short lines or hooks, at the ends of the letter strokes. Serifs assist the eye in moving from letter to letter and aid in reading comfort and speed. Serif typefaces can be used for main body text and headlines.

Sans serif means without serifs. Sans serif letters have clean, straight lines and a geometric appearance. These faces are primarily used for headlines, lists, charts, short blocks of text, and captions.

Display typefaces attract attention. They are often thick and bold. Display faces are primarily used for headlines, posters, and advertisements.

Script typefaces give words either a playful or an elegant look. Script letters might resemble calligraphy or look like they were written with a pen or brush. Script faces are most often used for announcements, headlines, and informal notices.

Symbols are sets of graphic marks such as stars and arrows. Symbols are often used as decorative ornaments or as markers in maps and charts.

Point Size and Line Spacing

Setting a block of type in the proper size and using the right amount of space between lines is essential not only for ensuring that text is easy to read but also for making sure that the text fits into an allotted space in your layout. Designers use units called "picas" and "points" when measuring type. There are 6 picas in 1 inch, 12 points in 1 pica, and 72 points in 1 inch.

The size of most typefaces can be measured, in points, from the top of the tallest letters, or "ascenders" (such as b, h, and l), to the bottom of the lowest letters, or "descenders" (such as g, p, and y). Different sizes of type should be used for headlines, text, and subheads.

Line spacing or **leading** (pronounced "ledding") is the distance in points between two lines of type. Leading is usually measured from the baseline, or bottom, of one line of type to the baseline of the next.

Most desktop publishing software automatically sets line spacing at 120 percent of type size. That is, if a designer selects 10-point type, the computer will automatically set 12-point leading. Designers record the relationship of point size to leading as "10/12" or "50/60" (pronounced "10 on 12," "50 on 60").

Many professional designers tighten leading to fit more text on a page or to give text a darker, denser look. Body text with a more open leading looks lighter and can be easier to read. Headlines of more than one line are often more readable when the leading is tightened.

Most page layout software can adjust leading to 1/10 of a point. This fine control assists the designer in **copyfitting** type into a given space on a page. Type size and leading are measured on a printed page with a special ruler called a "type gauge." Computer layout programs allow you to make measurements in printers' units, such as points and picas, as well as standard units, such as inches.

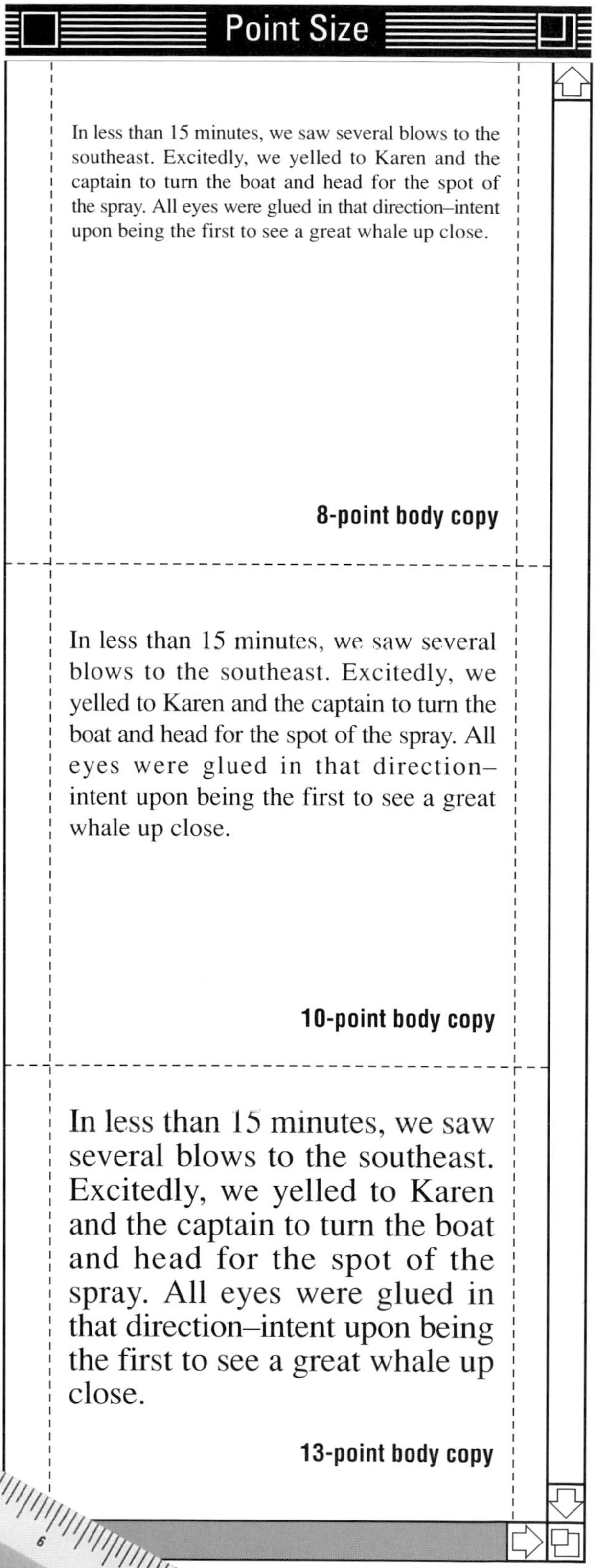

Point Size

In less than 15 minutes, we saw several blows to the southeast. Excitedly, we yelled to Karen and the captain to turn the boat and head for the spot of the spray. All eyes were glued in that direction–intent upon being the first to see a great whale up close.

8-point body copy

In less than 15 minutes, we saw several blows to the southeast. Excitedly, we yelled to Karen and the captain to turn the boat and head for the spot of the spray. All eyes were glued in that direction–intent upon being the first to see a great whale up close.

10-point body copy

In less than 15 minutes, we saw several blows to the southeast. Excitedly, we yelled to Karen and the captain to turn the boat and head for the spot of the spray. All eyes were glued in that direction–intent upon being the first to see a great whale up close.

13-point body copy

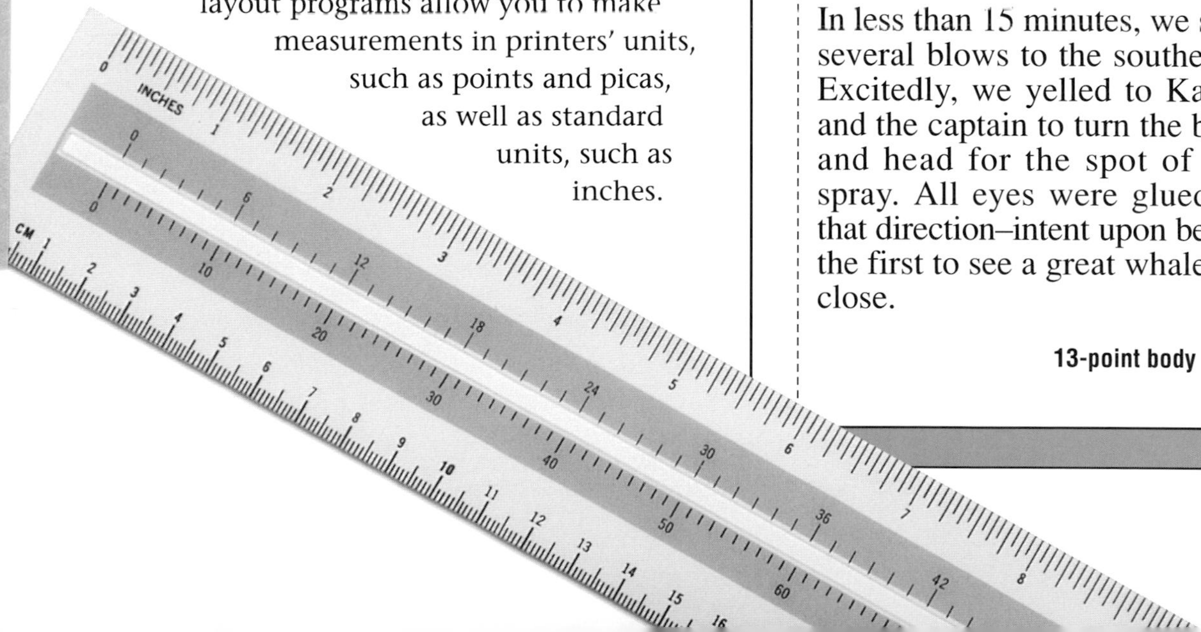

Leading Samples

In less than 15 minutes, we saw several blows to the southeast. Excitedly, we yelled to Karen and the captain to turn the boat and head for the spot of the spray. All eyes were glued in that direction–intent upon being the first to see a great whale up close.

10/10 leading

In less than 15 minutes, we saw several blows to the southeast. Excitedly, we yelled to Karen and the captain to turn the boat and head for the spot of the spray. All eyes were glued in that direction–intent upon being the first to see a great whale up close.

10/12 leading

In less than 15 minutes, we saw several blows to the southeast. Excitedly, we yelled to Karen and the captain to turn the boat and head for the spot of the spray. All eyes were glued in that direction–intent upon being the first to see a great whale up close.

10/17 leading

Type Terminology

Serif
Ascender
Eclipse
Baseline
Descender
Uppercase letter
Lowercase letters

Type Style

Style refers to special forms of a typeface such as boldface (thicker strokes), italic (slanted type), reverse (white type), and underline. Special type styles are used to emphasize words. Often boldface (as in this book) calls attention to words that are defined in a glossary. Italic type is usually used for foreign words and the titles of books and magazines. Reverse type must always be set against a dark background. Bold, italic, and reverse type are also used for headlines and subheads. As a rule, avoid underlined type, which sometimes looks messy and can distract a reader.

Alignment

"Alignment" refers to how a block of type lines up in a column. There are four principal alignments:

Left-aligned type lines up evenly on the left side of a column but is ragged, or uneven, on the right side. Left aligned type is commonly used for body copy, especially in newsletters.

Right-aligned, or ragged left, type lines up evenly on the right side of a column but not on the left side. Right aligned type is used only in special situations.

Center-aligned means that each line in a block of type is centered on a page or centered inside a column. Center-aligned type does not line up on the right or left side of a column. Centered type is frequently used for headlines, posters, announcements, and quotations.

Justified type lines up evenly on both the left and right sides of a column. Justified type is often used in books and newspapers. It gives a uniform, rectangular appearance to a publication.

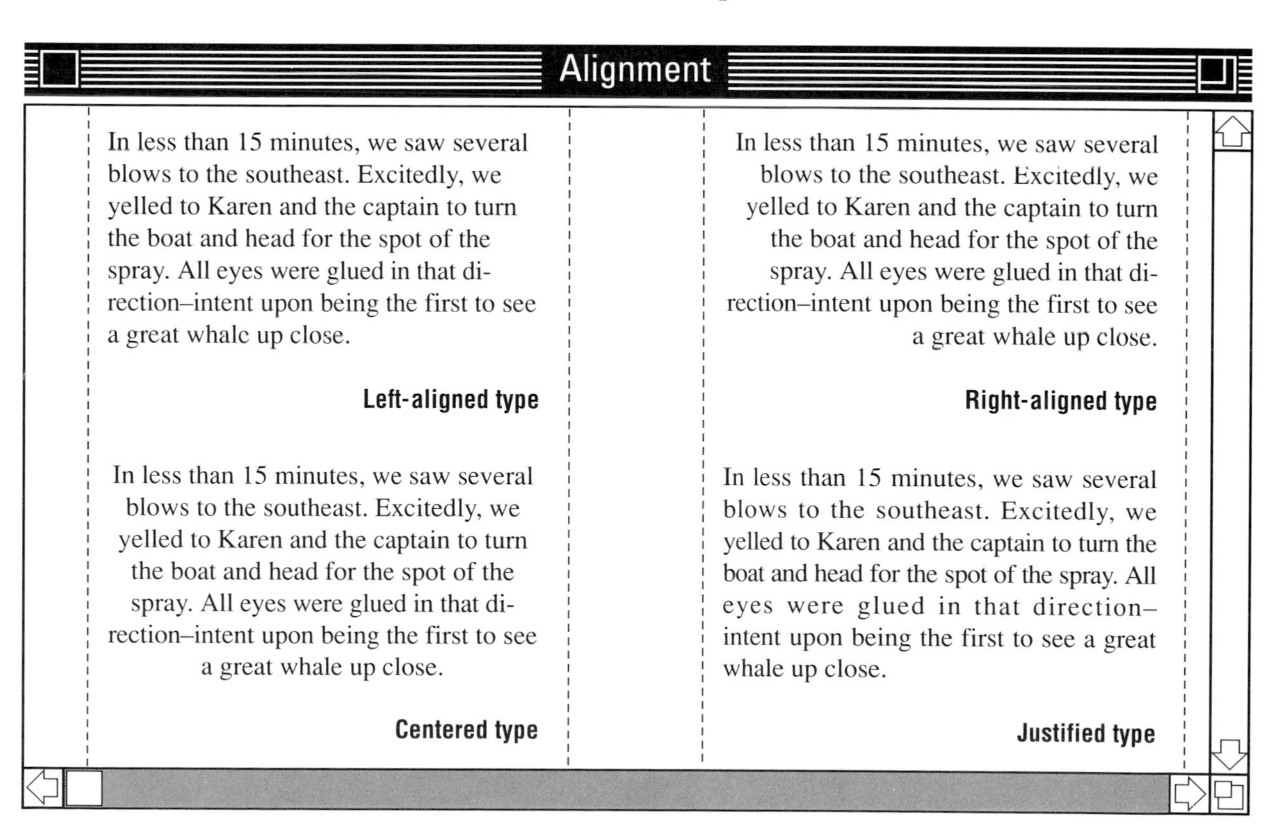

Indentation and Hyphenation

Paragraph indentation aids reading ease and story organization. Newsletter designers often set paragraph indents 1/16 or 1/8 inch from the left margin.

Most layout programs do automatic end-of-line hyphenation (word breaks) or allow you to hyphenate manually. Hyphenation gives text a clean, even appearance, especially in justified paragraphs. Avoid two or more end-of-line hyphens in a row, however, and don't break words in headlines and subheads.

Advanced Formatting

Page layout and drawing programs offer many advanced formatting tools. Advanced formatting gives you control over the space between letters, words, and paragraphs and allows you to stretch or narrow a typeface. Advanced formatting is used to refine and polish the appearance of body text and to create customized headlines. Advanced techniques include tracking, kerning, paragraph spacing, condensing, and expanding.

Tracking is a formatting technique used to tighten or loosen all the space between words and letters in a block of text. Tracking can be used for copyfitting or to increase the readability of type. Type with tight tracking will look darker and denser and will take up less space in a layout. Type with loose tracking will take up more space on a page and will appear lighter.

Effective tracking will make a block of type look even instead of choppy. Designers can also use tracking to eliminate "widows"—short lines at the top of a column of type.

Kerning allows the designer to control the amount of space between individual letters. Sometimes, letter pairs, such as **To** and **AC**, don't fit together well. Designers use kerning to tighten or loosen letter pairs for improved appearance or copyfitting.

In kerning, a unit of measurement called an "em" is used to describe the change in space between letters. One em is equal to the square of the point size of the type being used. That is, if a headline is set in 72-point type, one em is 72 points high and 72 points wide. Page layout programs let

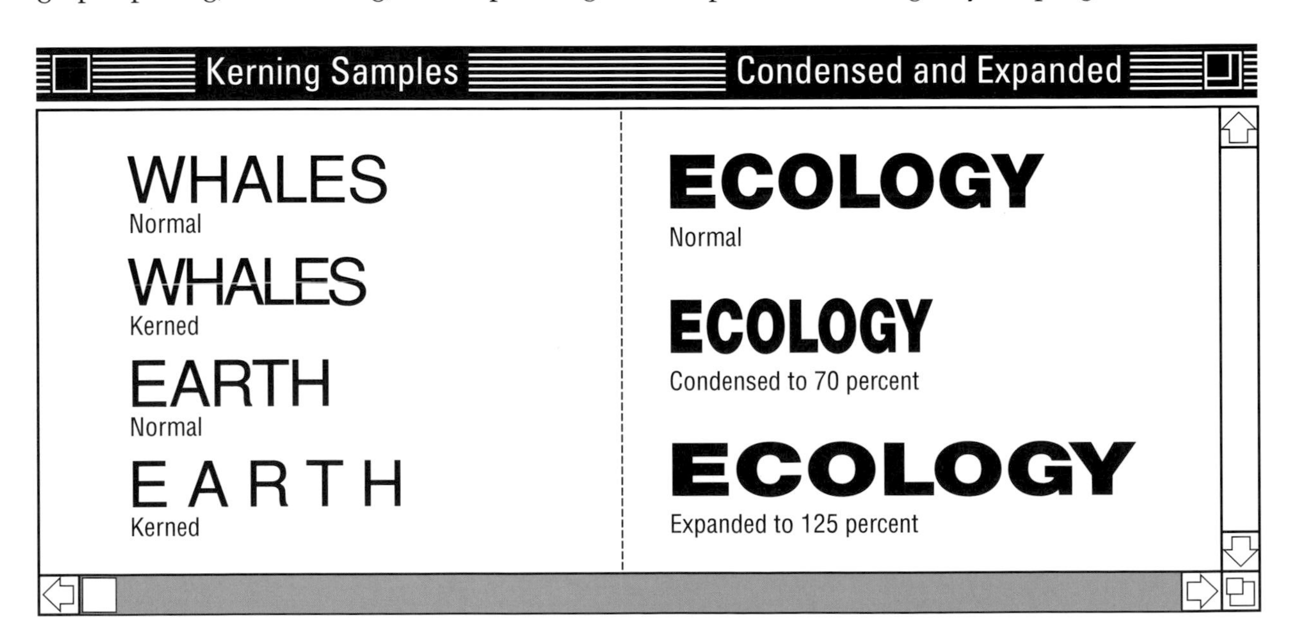

you kern space between letters in 1/10- and 1/100-em increments. Most page layout programs have an auto-kerning feature that will automatically tighten hundreds of letter pairs to make them look more professional.

Paragraph spacing allows you to increase or decrease, in small increments, the distance between paragraphs in a block of text. Paragraph spacing is an important technique used in copyfitting.

Headlines can be made more dynamic or inviting by *condensing* or *expanding* type width, while leaving type height, or point size, the same. In some layout programs, type can be condensed to 25 percent of its original width or expanded to 250 percent. A small change—condensing type to 97 percent of its original width, for instance—can often help in copyfitting.

Special Effects

All advanced drawing programs and some page layout programs allow you to apply special effects to type. Special effect techniques include masking (placing an image *inside* type), placing type along a curve (useful for logos and advertisements), and perspective, or "zoom type," which makes letters appear three dimensional.

Stroke-and-fill is a special technique that involves separating headline type into an outer "stroke" and an inner "fill" of colors, shades, or patterns. Scaling, another special effect technique, means reducing or enlarging type to any size, while still retaining the sharpness of the letterforms.

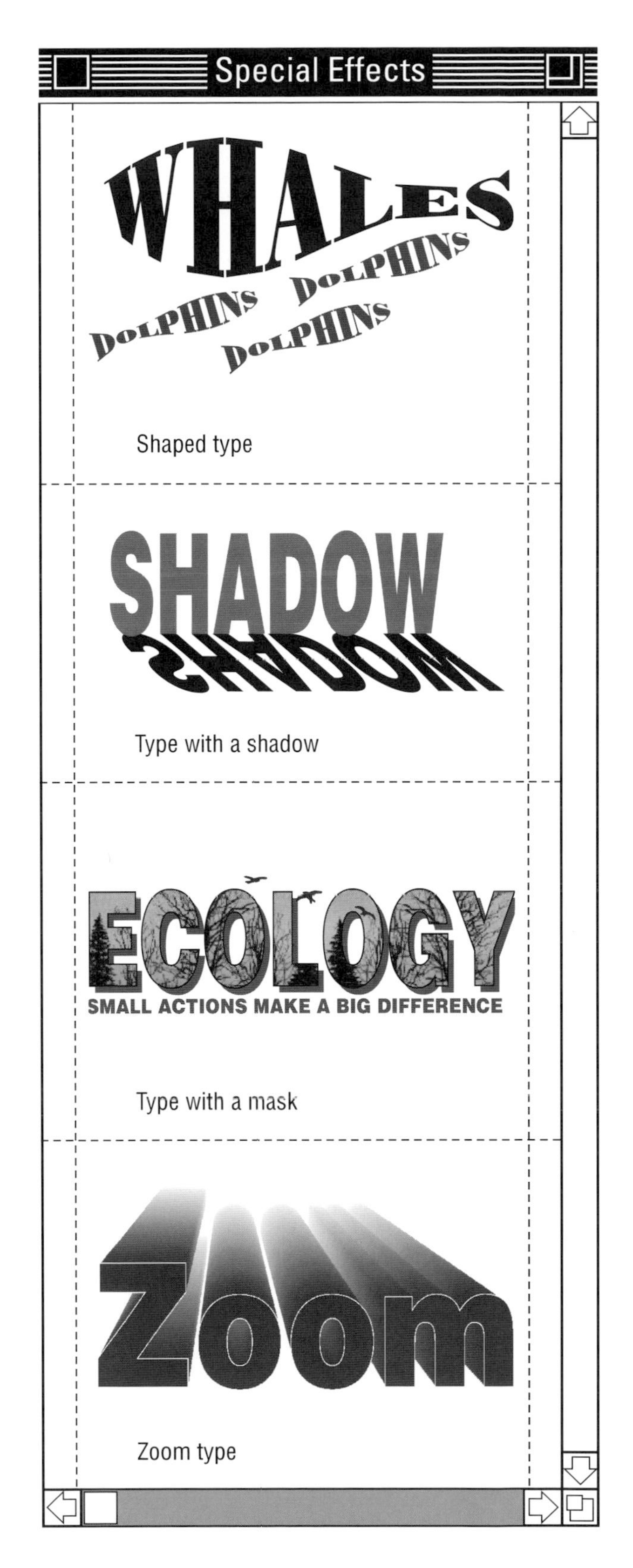

15 items 1,370K in disk 46K available

Scanning software lets the desktop publisher apply numerous special effects to artwork and photographs. *Opposite page:* A clip art whale (left); illustrating by hand (center)

Chapter Seven

ILLUSTRATION

Illustrations enhance the writer's message. They spark interest, attract readers, and work with stories to help produce an effective publication.

The computer enables the desktop publisher to insert many different kinds of images into a layout. Pictures can be reproduced with photographic realism, manipulated for special effect, or drawn with the precision of an engineering blueprint. In the past, advanced graphic techniques were only available to specialists. But with electronic page layout and drawing software, anyone with interest and patience can learn to produce exciting and attractive images.

Computer graphic artists use four types of images: line art, photographs, drawing program graphics, and painting program graphics. Often, a designer combines two or more different kinds of images into a single graphic.

Line Art

Line art consists of single-color drawings made with pen and ink, pencils, charcoal, or other similar media on paper. Line art is expressive, simple, and to the point. Animals, people, buildings, vehicles, and cartoon figures are often presented with line art, as are diagrams, logos, and decorative borders. Line art drawn by hand can be scanned into a computer layout or pasted into a layout by traditional keylining methods.

Desktop publishers can also buy clip art: illustrations created by professional artists that can be copied and used without written permission. Clip art books contain drawings that can be scanned into a computer or that can be photocopied and pasted into a layout by hand. Clip art software offers illustrations that can be called up on the computer screen and set into a page layout program.

Photographs

The primary goal when working with photographs is to faithfully reproduce colors and shades of gray from the original photograph into the printed publication. Desktop designers work with three types of photographs: continuous tone, **halftone**, and color.

Continuous tone images are black-and-white photographs printed directly from film negatives. Look at a black-and-white photo under a magnifying glass and you will see how different shades of gray blend together to form the image. Printers do not reproduce continuous tone photographs by using different shades of gray ink, though.

The "Ecology Action" photographer uses a magnifying glass to examine photographs printed on a contact sheet.

Instead, printers and desktop publishers change continuous tone photographs into halftones. Halftone photographs are reproduced with black ink alone.

Halftones are made up of thousands of small, evenly spaced black dots that vary in size. When printed on a white background, the black dots appear to merge and look like shades of gray. All the black-and-white photographs in this book are halftones. You can turn continuous tone photographs into halftones with a scanner and a laser printer or imagesetter or by taking your photographs to a commercial print shop.

Color photographs can also be turned into black-and-white halftones using a scanner and a high-quality printer. But if you want to reproduce a photograph in full-color, the image must be processed by a method called **four-color separation**. Four-color processing separates the millions of colors in a photograph into only four colors: cyan (blue), magenta (red), yellow, and black. When printed, the four colors combine to reproduce the original colors of the photograph on paper.

Color separation is expensive and requires sophisticated equipment. Some computers can separate photographs, but computer technology is just beginning to compete with traditional color separation methods.

Scanners

Desktop users can place images into a layout design either through traditional paste-up methods or by the use of a scanner. Scanners turn images into digital information that can be read by a computer and displayed on a monitor. The designer can then electronically edit or apply special effects to the image on the screen.

Scanners use a beam of light to make a map of an image. A scanner analyzes each

Halftones are photographs made up of dots of varying sizes.

section of a picture, taking between 5,000 and 90,000 light readings per square inch. Each reading receives a number, with different numbers for white, black, shades of gray, and—with the most expensive scanners—different colors. These numbers form a digital map, or bit map, that can be displayed on the computer monitor.

Scanners are rated by their bit-mapping capabilities. One-bit scanners are good for reproducing line art but not photographs. An eight-bit scanner can read up to 256 shades of gray and can faithfully produce photographic images. Top-of-the-line 24-bit scanners can read millions of colors and are used for making four-color separations. Some scanning software can flop (reverse) images, sharpen images, or create negative images.

After you scan an image, you will need to store it on disk. Image processing software offers several different systems, called "file formats," for storing scanned images. The two most common file formats are PICT (for picture) and TIFF (Tag Image File Format).

Most desktop publishers find that TIFF is the most versatile file format. The TIFF format allows you to apply numerous special effects to stored images, whereas other file formats are more limited.

This progressive magnification shows that a scanned photograph is really a bit-mapped image.

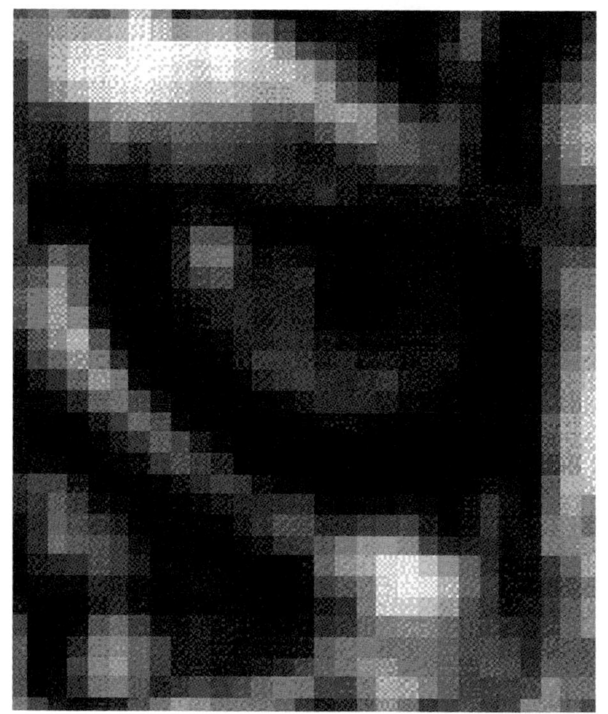

Computer Illustration

Desktop publishers can create their own illustrations on the computer using drawing and painting software. With a computer illustration program, nonartists can learn to produce high-quality graphics, while experienced artists can expand and enhance their skills.

Drawing software lets you produce high-resolution images that can be easily resized and imported into your page layout software. Drawing program graphics consist of geometric objects such as lines, circles, and rectangles. Most national newspapers and magazines use drawing programs to create charts, graphs, logos, and realistic illustrations.

A flatbed scanner fits on a desktop.

Creating the "Ecology Action" Logo

15 items | 1,370K in disk | 46K available

1. Scan a clip art Earth image.

2. Remove the latitude and longitude lines from the Earth using a painting program eraser tool.

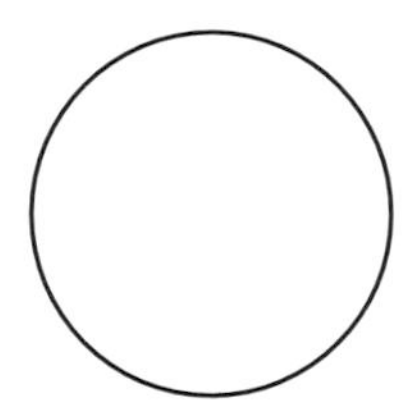

3. Create a circle the same size as the Earth image.

4. Shade the circle from white to black to show dimension and to give the illusion of reflected sunlight.

5. Superimpose the Earth and the shaded circle (place one on top of the other).

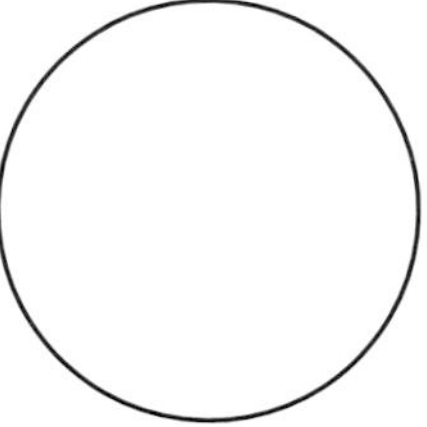

6. Create a circle slightly larger than the Earth image.

7. Set and format the "Ecology Action" motto.

8. Curve the type along the path of the large circle.

9. Position the motto over the Earth image.

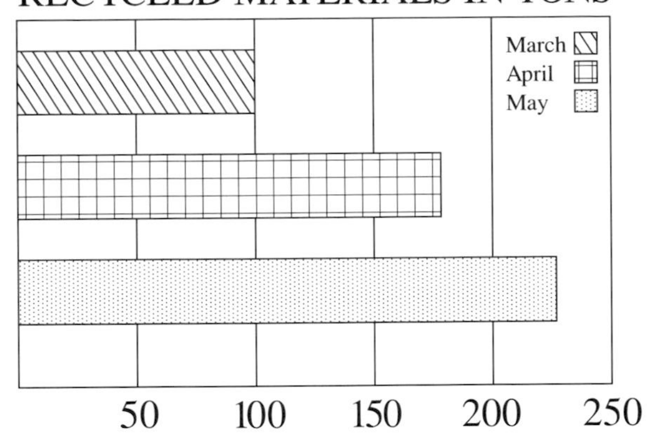

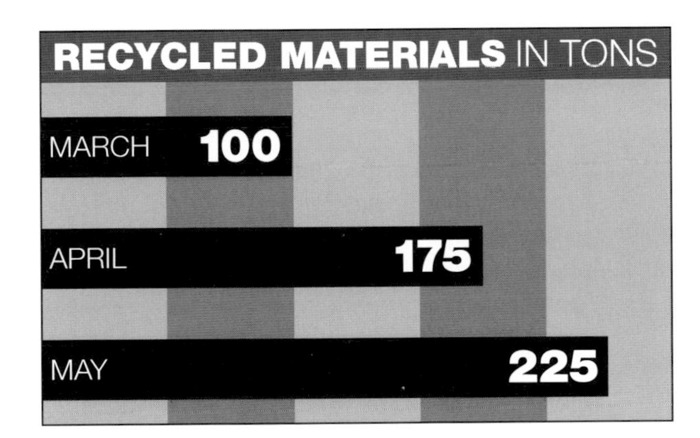

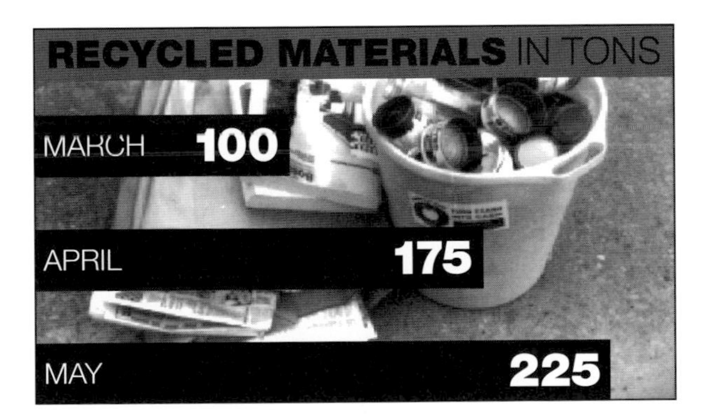

Graphs and charts can be simple or complex. The first two graphs shown above were created with page layout software. The third graph includes a scanned image.

There are two kinds of drawing programs: basic and PostScript. A basic drawing program can be used to create simple graphics, charts, and diagrams. PostScript, the most powerful graphics art software available, can be used to produce high-quality images as well as numerous special effects. PostScript programs can rotate and skew images (useful for three-dimensional effects), make mirror images, create curves, join type to a curved path, and produce shadow effects.

Painting program images are made up of a map of square pixels (like a checkerboard of tiles). A circle or line created in a painting program will look like row of adjoining tiles. Painting software includes a tool called an eraser that allows you to edit scanned line art one pixel at a time. Different paintbrushes allow you to create and blend textures and patterns.

Painting graphics have disadvantages, though, including distortion when you resize the art in your page layout and low-resolution print quality. Painting graphics sometimes have jagged edges, even when outputted on a high-resolution printer.

With desktop publishing, what you see on the computer screen is what you'll get on the printed page. *Opposite page:* A two-page spread on the computer screen (center)

Chapter Eight

LAYOUT

A layout is the arrangement of type and illustrations on a surface called a "pasteboard." A good-looking, dynamic layout is built in steps. The five principal steps in the layout process are establishing a page format, building a framework of columns, placing text and graphic images into the column framework, copyfitting the text, and decorating and polishing the layout.

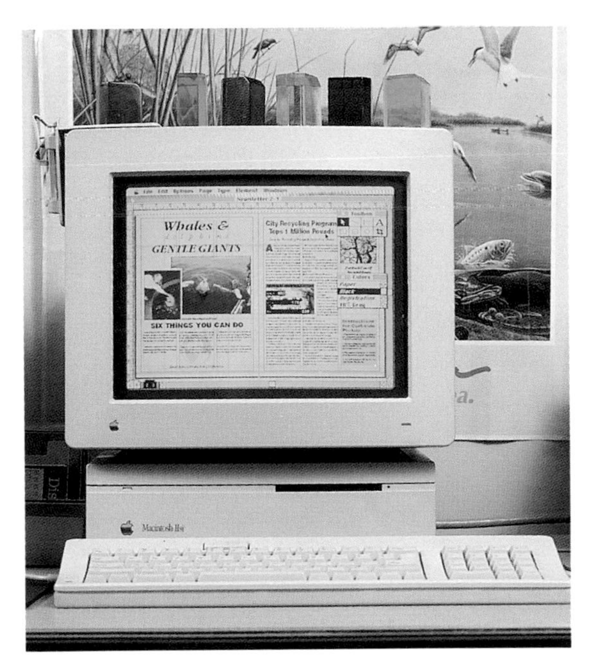

Page Format

In Chapter Five, we discussed setting the page format, or page specifications, for your newsletter. Page layout software can automatically create pages at different sizes. Decide if you want your layout to have a vertical or horizontal orientation, or shape. Add margins around the edge of each page.

Columns

Next add column guides to create a frame, or grid, for your text and artwork. Columns shorten the length of each line of type and cause less eye strain for the reader. Most newsletters have between two and four columns per page.

High-quality photographs enhance your text and make your publication more attractive.

Page layout software will let you create multiple columns and specify how much space you want between columns. This space, called the "gutter," is usually about 1/5 inch wide. Both column and margin guides will appear as light dotted lines on your computer screen, but they won't show up on the printed page.

Text and Graphics

Publications are built by arranging three principal elements: graphics, headlines, and text. Text and graphics will generally be imported into your layout software from other programs. Headlines and decorative elements are usually created in the page layout program itself.

Graphic elements—like your masthead (newsletter title and logo), illustrations, and photographs—are usually positioned first. Next, using page layout typing tools, you create headlines. Finally, the formatted text for each story is imported into your layout and threaded into columns. That is, the text will fill in the blank spaces between the headlines and images.

Try to organize all the elements in your layout without crowding. Remember to let the page breathe. Make sure that one element is not butting up too close to another. The use of white space will relieve eye strain for the reader.

Parts of a Newsletter

15 items   1,370K in disk   46K available

Body text includes informational articles, lists, and call-outs.

Each story has a **headline** that is brief, bold, and to the point. Headline type is usually created with page layout rather than word processing software.

A **caption,** or cutline, describes a photograph or illustration. Captions are often set in italic type.

Bylines at the beginning or end of each story identify the writer.

Include **page numbers** at the top or bottom of each page (except page 1). Most page layout programs have a page numbering feature that saves you time and positions page numbers precisely.

A **masthead** consists of your newsletter title and logo. The masthead remains the same for each issue. Below the masthead are the issue number and date, both of which will change with each issue.

Graphics include photographs, illustrations, charts, and decorative elements.

Creating the "Ecology Action" Page Layout

1. Set margin guides.

2. Set column guides.

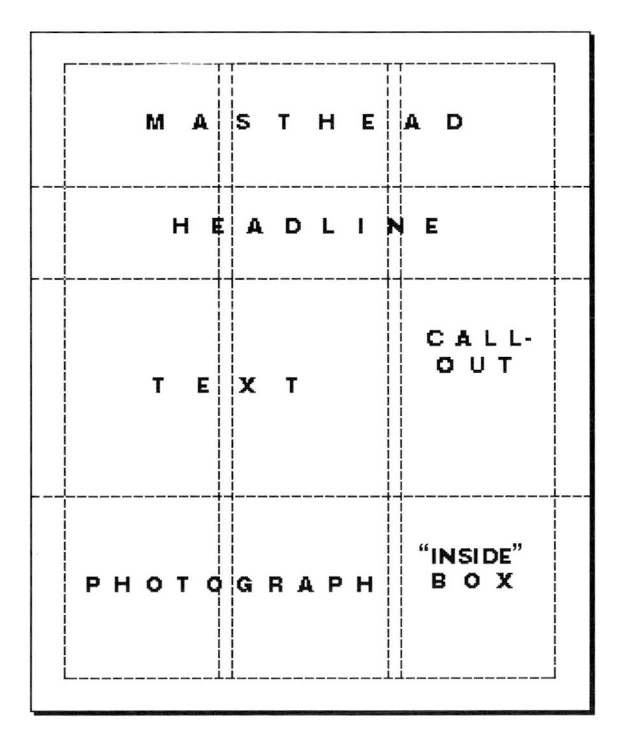

3. Block out the major elements on each page.

4. Import graphic elements and create headlines.

ECOLOGY Action

WATER ★ AIR ★ LAND ★ LIFE

ISSUE 1 SPRING 1992

Protecting the Gentle Giants in Our Seas

"Look for puffs of mist along the horizon," shouted our whale watch guide, Karen Smyth, "that means whales!" Whales are mammals like humans and need to inhale and exhale air. The exhale breath of a whale blows air and water out as a fine spray."

In less than 15 minutes, we saw several blows to the southeast. Excitedly, we yelled to the captain to turn the boat and head for the spot of the spray. All eyes were glued in that direction–intent upon being the first to see a great whale up close.

For several minutes all was calm. Did they swim away from us fearing capture or harm from our noisy, growling engine? As our patience wore thin, the ocean erupted. A spiraling, soaring creature exploded out of the sea as if wanting to fly, with 12-foot flippers extended against the sky. As our whale crashed back into its ocean home, it sent out a fountain of spray 20 feet high that washed across our faces. We had witnessed one of nature's most awesome sights–a breaching 40-foot long, 40-ton humpback whale. For the rest of the day, we were in the company of whales. At times they "played" with our boat by diving under the hull or slapped their flippers as if waving to us.

Humpback whales spend the summer months living and feeding in the cold waters of the North Atlantic Ocean. In the fall months, the whales migrate thousands of miles to the Caribbean Sea and give birth

continued on page 4

"Humpback whale populations have grown since laws banning hunting were passed...but they're not saved yet."

INSIDE

5. Import and copyfit text and decorate and detail the layout.

With the basic elements in place, print a hard copy of your layout and critique it for balance, organization, and errors. After this review, polish the layout by copyfitting the text and adding decorative elements.

Copyfitting

Copyfitting means making sure your text fits in the space available in your layout. If your text is too long or too short to fit precisely, use the following methods to copyfit the text:

- edit the story (adding or deleting text, as needed)
- resize the pictures
- change the type point size
- change the leading
- change the spacing between paragraphs
- change the tracking
- slightly condense or expand the width of your typeface (97 to 103 percent, for instance)
- add more space between columns

Remember that sizing and spacing changes must be applied to all the type in your newsletter, not just to one story, or else the publication will appear uneven and unbalanced. Try not to leave empty space at the end of a story. Columns should be filled with text or graphics, unless space is left empty on purpose, as part of your newsletter design.

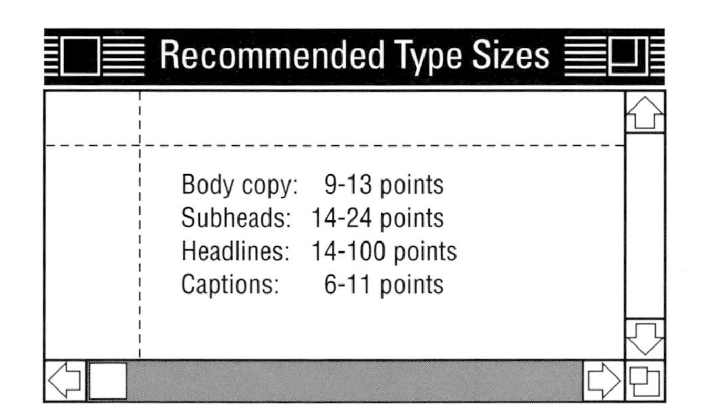
Recommended Type Sizes

Body copy:	9-13 points
Subheads:	14-24 points
Headlines:	14-100 points
Captions:	6-11 points

Whales &
d o l p h i n s
GENTLE GIANTS

Naturalist Karen Smyth and friends

SIX THINGS YOU CAN DO

• Support the protection of coastal wetlands. Coastal wetlands are the primary sources of food for life in the ocean. Currents carry this food to areas where whales live and feed.

• Write letters asking seafood companies to find alternatives to fishing techniques that trap dolphins with commercial fish.

• Don't use pesticides and chemicals for lawns and gardens. Pesticides are poison for all forms of life. There are many organic alternatives for growing healthy green spaces.

• Support environmental research and education by joining and actively working with local and national ecology organizations.

• Write letters to local, state and national government officials to support the highest level of sewage treatment and the cleanup of urban rivers and ocean harbors.

• Recycle! Recycling waste reduces pollution from dumps. Chemicals from dumps leak into water supplies and flow to the ocean.

Small Actions Make A Big Difference

2

Be sure to include page numbers, except on page 1.

Decorating and Polishing the Layout

You can use page layout drawing tools to create special effects such as shadows, frames, rules (lines), and other design elements that will make your publication more interesting. Frames and boxes can give a page or a column a unified appearance. Lines, boxes, shadows, and other decorations should be consistent in thickness and tone.

Using color and shades of gray can help to organize and highlight information. A gray tint behind a column of type, for instance, will attract attention to the column.

City Recycling Program Tops 1 Million Pounds

Save for Recycling Because Recycling Saves

At seven o'clock, an unusual looking truck turned the corner onto my street. Just a new type of garbage truck, I thought. But in a few moments I found out I was wrong. In place of a deafening groan as mechanical jaws crushed tons of garbage, only the tinkle of breaking glass could be heard. Two men chased the truck on foot, running to the curb for loads of neatly wrapped newspaper, glass, and cans. To my surprise, several other residents braved the morning chill to see the big event. It was the first day of recycling in our town.

"It's about time" shouted Mary Issacs from her porch. "It's such a shame that this program wasn't started 10 years ago." "I hope they spend the money they save from the trash to plant a few new trees on our street or fix up the tot-lot for the kids," yelled Carmen Miraflores as he carried his morning paper and a bottle of apple juice home from the corner store.

"Garbage collecting in Somerville has taken a new turn: recycling. It's great after 27 years of doing the other," said a smiling Jim Mendes, who is a worker on the trucks. The residents of Somerville agree. By May, the Recycling program had collected over one million pounds of glass, paper and cans in its first three months of operation.

Environmental officials from the city have been elated. City Representative Louis Vittelli gave four reason why recycling is so important.

Saving Energy

It takes a lot less energy to make a new product from recycled materials that from raw materiels. The energy savings for aluminum are 95%, steel cans 55%, and paper 70%.

Saving Limited Natural Resources

In the last 30 years, our throwaway society is rapidly using up the earth's limited supply of resources. Recycling can save resources by using the ones we have over and over again.

Economic Savings

For every ton of glass, paper or cans that is recycled, Somerville now receives about $30.00. At the current recycling rate, the city will save over $60,000 a year.

A Healthier Environment

Garbage has to go somewhere. "Throw away" means that garbage is going into a dump or incinerator in our town or another community. By recycling we reduce the pollution from dumps and burning.

Although the program is only three months old, recycling really isn't a new idea. Nature has been recycling successfully for millions of years. By understanding the laws of nature, we can begin to work with the earth not against it.

Students interested in helping increase public participation can pick up posters and leaflets in Room A119 for local distribution. – *by Tara Green*

For Each Ton Of Recycled Paper

- *17 mature trees are saved*
- *Enough energy is conserved to heat the average American house for six months*
- *7000 gallons of water are saved*
- *60 pounds less of air pollution is produced*

Instructions for Curbside Pickup

1. Paper including newsprint, magazines and envelopes should be tied and bundled or placed in a paper bag.
2. All colors of glass and metal cans should be mixed together in a cotnainer. A sturdy box or trash can is best.
3. Place paper and glass/cans on curbside about three feet away from regular trash.
4. Recycling pickup will be on your regualr trash collection day.

3

Charts and graphs help readers better understand statistics and technical information. Gray tints and boxes highlight special information.

Most page layout software can automatically "wrap" text around an image, creating a unique look. The distance from the text to the graphic is called the "stand-off."

You can also use page layout software to create "drop caps" that will attract a reader's attention. A drop cap, or "initial cap," is the first letter of a story or article. Drop caps are often larger or more stylized than the rest of the text. They lead the reader's eye into the story.

Call-outs or "pull quotes" are quotations or segments of body text duplicated in a large point size and placed prominently on a page. Call-outs are used to catch the reader's eye and to highlight parts of a story. Call-out passages are usually set in boldface or italic, in 14- to 18-point type. They should be positioned in your layout so that the reader sees the call-out before coming across the same passage in the text.

SKY WATCH

This month's Sky Watch meeting will feature a field trip to the Museum of Science for a multimedia presentation by Taylor St. Clair on comets, meteors and the aurora. Mr. St. Clair will show slides from an expedition he lead in 1986 into the Andes Mountains of Peru to photograph Halley's Comet and record Native American myths and legends. Date: June 9,1992.

Sky Watch Alert! Look towards the western sky an hour after sunset for a rare conjunction of the planets Jupiter, Mars, and Venus. The planets will appear as starlike points of light in the shape of a triangle. The brightest is Venus, next is Jupiter, then Mars (which will appear slightly red). Anyone wishing to see the planets through the school's telescope should see Mr. Williams in room B109.

ADOPT A WHALE

continued from page 1

to young calves in the winter. Calves at birth weigh 1,000 pounds and require 50 gallons of mom's milk per day! In the spring, the whale families migrate north. Before day's end we would see several adult humpbacks with young calves by their side.

"Humpback whale populations have grown since laws banning hunting were passed...but, they're not saved yet," explained Karen. Stormy Mayo, director of the Center for Coastal Studies in Provincetown, Massachusetts, wrote "The sea is for us and for the great whales both our nest and our garden, but upon it we pour hundreds of thousands of barrels of oil yearly; we dispose willfully the refuse of our society as toxic wastes and as sewage by the million gallon lot...."

Destruction of the ocean habitat is the greatest current threat to the survival of whales. Another is the trapping of dolphins (also members of the whale family) in fishing nets. In the tropical eastern Pacific, 80,000 dolphins die annually due to tuna fishing. On page two of this newsletter are some ideas on what you can do to help protect whales and dolphins.

You can help support whale and dolphin research through a program named the Whale Adoption Project. The project is sponsored by the International Wildlife Coalition in Falmouth, Massachusetts. Each whale has a pattern of black and white marks its tail fins that are unique to that whale–much like human fingerprints. Using this characteristic, hundreds of whales have been identified, named, and are observed yearly as they migrate along the coasts. Names include Lightning, Feather, Scratch, and Cloud. If you are interested, contact our office (Room A119) for an application form. Adopters receive a photograph of their whale, a whale calendar, and a year's subscription to WhaleWatch newsletter for updates on the activities and location of adopted whales. Adoption fee is $15.00. – *by Tony Robinson*

NEXT ISSUE

Wolves
River Clean-up
Poster Contest

4

Notice how the text wraps around the "Adopt-A-Whale" logo.

Cropping and scaling are used to insure that images fit properly within your layout. Cropping is the technique of "cutting off" unwanted or unneeded parts of an image. You might crop a picture to highlight one individual or viewpoint or to make the image fit your layout. Page layout software can electronically crop scanned images. Cropping does not permanently remove the unwanted sections of the photograph, however. Pictures can be uncropped and recropped as necessary.

Scaling is the method of reducing and enlarging an image to fit within a defined space. Suppose an 8-by-10-inch photograph must fit into a 4-by-5 inch space. The photograph must be scaled down, or reduced, by 50 percent. All page layout software programs let you scale scanned images. Be aware that a photograph that has been enlarged electronically might have a poorer resolution than the original.

Desktop publishers who don't own scanners often leave a blank space or box in their layouts to show where a photograph or hand-drawn illustration will be inserted. Those without scanners can go to a commercial print shop to have photographs cropped, scaled, and turned into halftones.

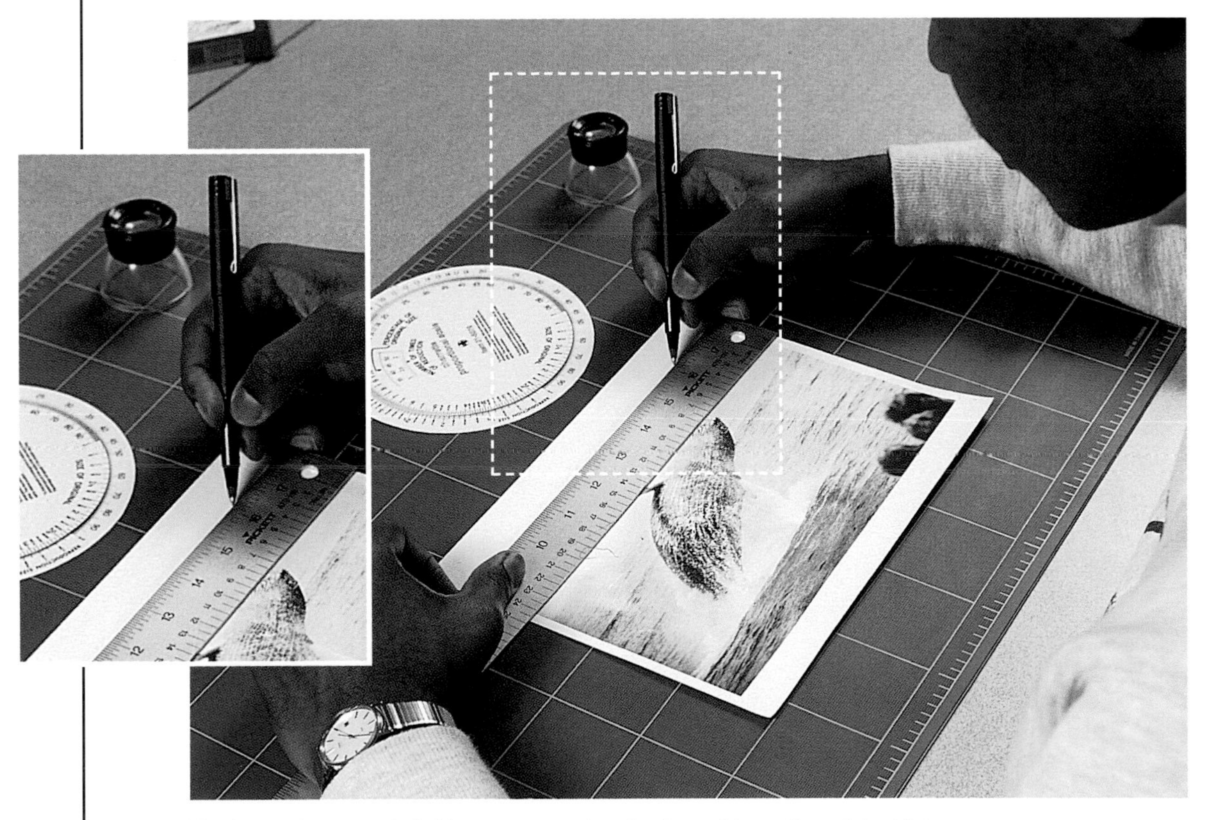

The inset photograph (left) was cropped and enlarged from the original image.

Review the outputted pages with a critical eye. *Opposite page:* Changes to your layout can be printed with ease and speed.

Chapter Nine

The Camera-Ready Mechanical

When your newsletter layout is finished, print out a hard copy and proof it for errors. Rearrange the type and graphics until you are satisfied with your design.

Since imagesetters produce better quality type and halftones than desktop laser printers, many desktop publishers take their page layout disk to a service bureau for imagesetting. By using a device called a **modem**, you can also send your layout to a service bureau over the telephone lines. The final layout, outputted on an imagesetter or laser printer and prepared for the commercial print shop, is called the **camera-ready mechanical.**

If you on are a tight budget, you can take a simple black-and-white mechanical to a copy shop for photocopying. Commercial printing costs more, but yields a better-looking publication. You will need to provide the commercial printer with certain instructions, such as how many copies of your newsletter to print, what kind of paper to use, and where to add color to your publication.

Four-Color Printing

15 items 1,370K in disk 46K available

Full-color photographs are reproduced in publications by a complex process called four-color separation. The four-color process uses four different inks: cyan (blue), magenta (red), yellow, and black. Mixing these inks in different proportions produces millions of colors.

To print a photo in full color, the image must first be "separated," or broken down, into the four basic colors. During printing, the four inks combine to reproduce the colors of the original photograph. With special software, computers can do quality four-color separation, but most desktop users give color photographs to a commercial print shop for separation.

Cyan

Magenta

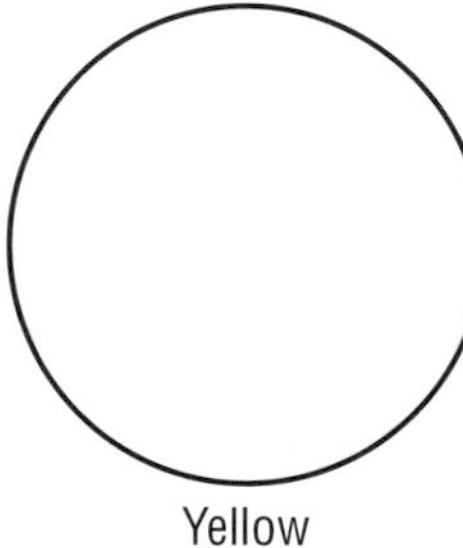

Yellow

Black

A printer operates a four-color press (bottom). The colors shown in the circles (top), when printed together, will create a full-color image of the man's head and shoulders.

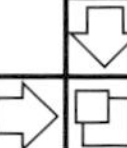

Adding Color

Color adds an exciting visual element to a publication that can attract, relax, or inspire the reader. One of the most common techniques for adding color is called "spot color." Spot color is the application of one, two, or three colors, in addition to black, to a publication. You might choose green for your masthead, headlines, and borders, for instance, while printing the rest of the newsletter in black ink.

To add spot color, designers use the Pantone Matching System, a set of more than 1,000 different color inks, each with an assigned number. The designer marks the elements of a layout that will receive an extra color by writing on an **overlay**, a clear piece of film or tissue covering the camera-ready mechanical. The commercial printer follows the designer's instructions and prints spot color in the publication where indicated.

PostScript drawing programs and page layout software contain electronic versions of the Pantone Matching System. Thus, the desktop user can scroll through the selection of Pantone inks and designate spot color for type, lines, or graphics right on the computer screen. Imagesetters and laser printers can print out film overlays for each color, with spot color shown in the appropriate position.

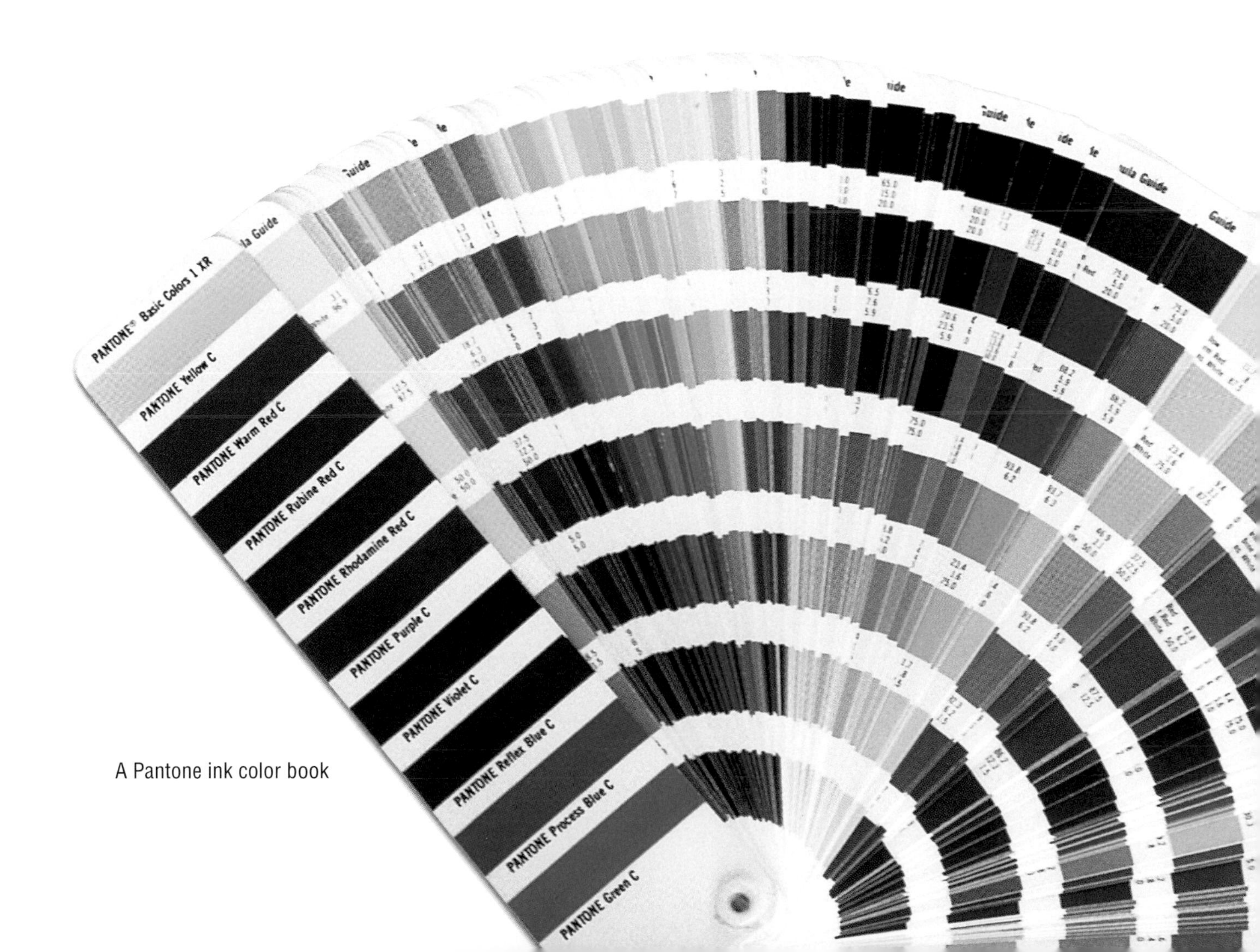

A Pantone ink color book

A clear film overlay shows where spot color will appear in a publication.

The Imposition

Before your publication can be printed, layout pages must be grouped in a special arrangement called an **imposition.** The imposition ensures that the newsletter pages will be in the correct order when they are printed and folded.

The ecology newsletter is composed of four 8½-by-11-inch pages. Pages 1 and 4 are placed on one 11-by-17-inch imposition board and pages 2 and 3 on another.

The two boards will be printed back-to-back, with pages 1 and 4 on one side of an 11-by-17-inch sheet and pages 2 and 3 on the other. When the printed sheet is folded in half, it will form an 8½-by-11-inch news-letter with the pages ordered correctly.

Printing two pages on one side of a single sheet is called "two-up printing." Impositions can be two-up, four-up, or greater, depending on the size of the printing press and length of the publication.

Most imposition boards will include lines called crop marks that show where the printed page will be trimmed. Crop marks are usually not needed on 8½-by-11 or 11-by-17-inch pages, however, since these are standard page sizes commonly used by printers. Odd size pages will need crop marks.

If you are printing in more than one color, you will also need registration marks, small crosses and circles drawn on both your overlays and your imposition boards. Registration marks insure that the imposition boards and overlays line up evenly—so that spot color will be printed precisely where you want it. Most page layout software allows you to add registration marks.

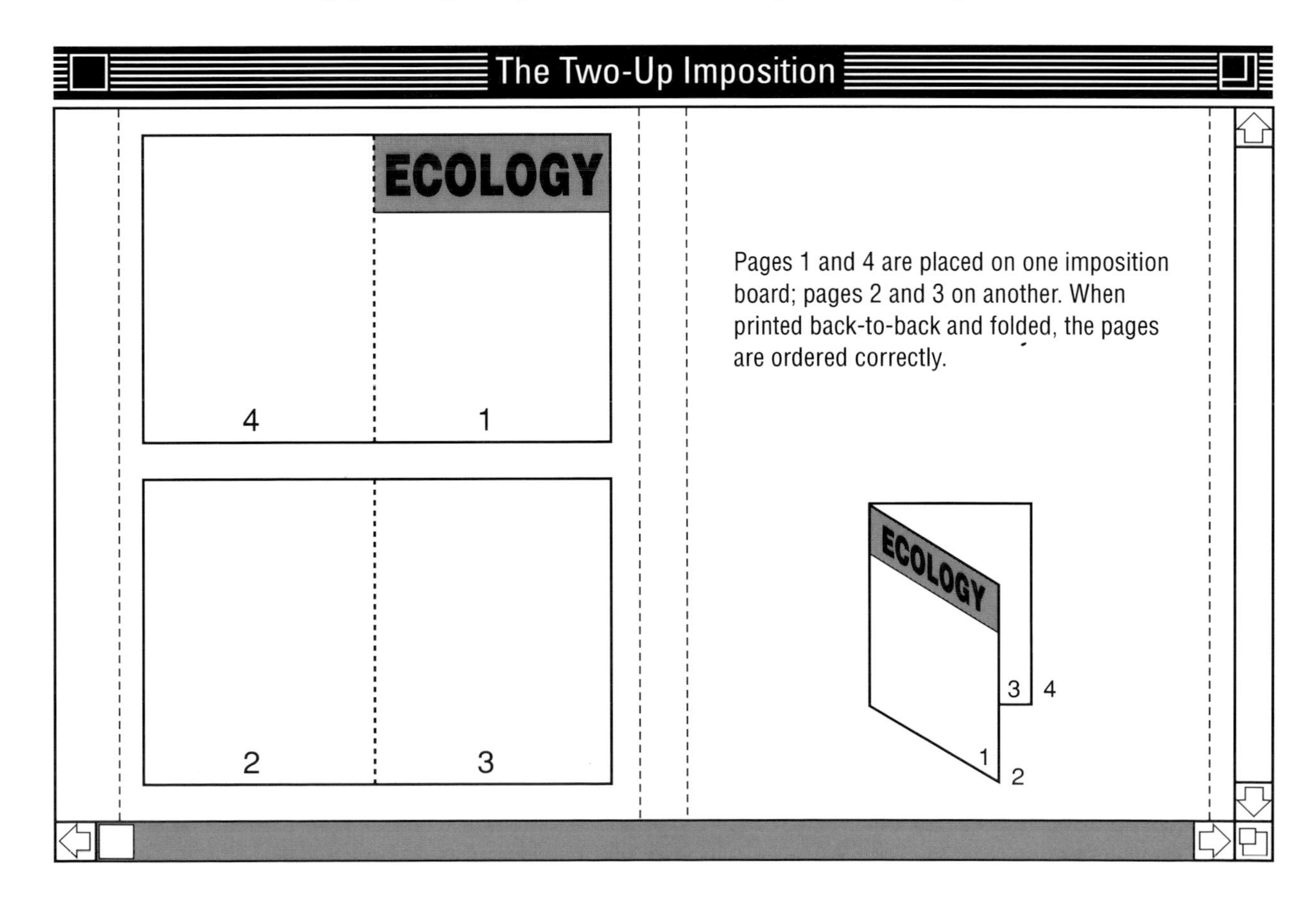

Loading paper into a press at a commercial print shop

The Finished Newsletter

When completed, the camera-ready mechanical boards will be given to a commercial printer (or photocopy shop) for reproduction. After your publication is printed and distributed, ask for feedback from your readers. Don't fear criticism—use the feedback to learn how you can improve your writing, illustrations, and design to create a better publication.

Successful desktop publishers build their skills by thorough research, observation, and experimentation. They take risks, use bold designs, and pay close attention to the fine details of alignment and composition.

Desktop publishing is called an "enabling technology" because it gives anyone the power to publish without expensive equipment and outside specialists. No matter what career you choose, a computer publishing system will improve your ability to create and communicate with clarity and originality.

ECOLOGY
Protecting the Gentle Giants in Our Seas
INSIDE
ECOLOGY
Protecting the Gentle Giants in Our Seas

GLOSSARY

baseline: the bottom of a line of type. Only descenders, such as **j**, **y**, and **g**, reach below the baseline.

bit map: An image made up of a series of pixels

camera-ready mechanical: the outputted layout, prepared for the commercial print shop

central processing unit: the part of the computer that interprets and carries out software instructions

copyfitting: adjusting type and images so that text fits in the allotted space on a page

desktop publishing: using a computer to arrange text and images in a page layout

digital information: data represented by the digits 1 and 0, arranged in codes that can be read by a computer

disk drive: a device that reads digital information from computer disks

floppy disks: portable units that store digital information and software instructions

four-color separation: the process of breaking a full-color photograph down into four basic colors: cyan, magenta, yellow, and black

halftone: a photograph made up of tiny black dots that appear to merge and simulate shades of gray

hard disk: a metallic platter that stores digital information

hardware: the mechanical and electronic components in a computer system

import: to transfer information from one computer program into another

imposition: a special arrangement for pages of a newsletter or book prior to printing. The imposition insures that the pages will be ordered correctly when the publication is printed and folded.

keyboard: a device with keys for entering letters, numbers, and symbols into a computer. Keyboards are also used to edit information and to send instructions to the computer

leading: the amount of space between lines in a column of type

memory: the amount of information that a computer can process

modem: a device that allows you to send information from one computer to another using telephone lines

mouse: a small hand-held unit that allows you to select, move, and edit information on a computer screen

overlay: a piece of tissue or clear film placed over a camera-ready mechanical

pixels: small squares on a computer screen that can be turned on or off to create a map of words and images

resolution: the sharpness of a printed image, measured by the number of dots printed per inch

scanner: a machine that turns graphic images into digital information that can be read by a computer

software: electronic instructions that operate computer hardware and allow computer users to perform special tasks

typeface: a series of alphabet characters set in a specific design

typesetting: composing words and figures into a line of type of a certain size, face, leading, and column length

typography: the art of designing, choosing, and formatting type

INDEX

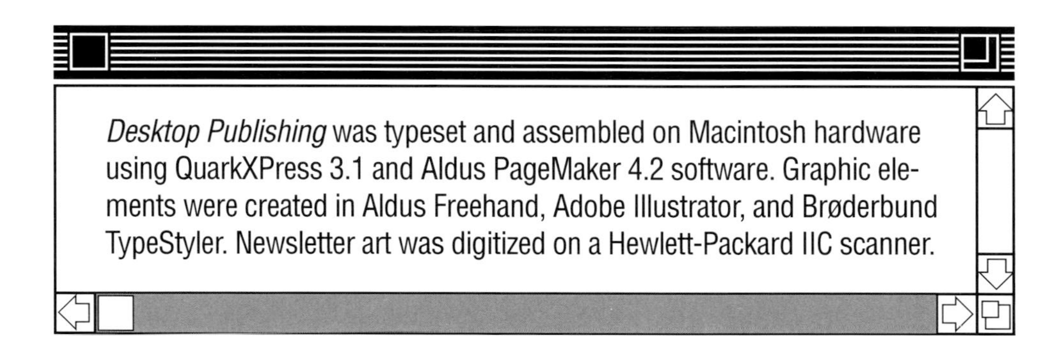
Desktop Publishing was typeset and assembled on Macintosh hardware using QuarkXPress 3.1 and Aldus PageMaker 4.2 software. Graphic elements were created in Aldus Freehand, Adobe Illustrator, and Brøderbund TypeStyler. Newsletter art was digitized on a Hewlett-Packard IIC scanner.

Acknowledgments

Photographs and illustrations by the author except: pp. 6, 21, 24, 30, 47, 54, 58, Patricia Garrity; pp. 7 (top), 8, Independent Picture Service; pp. 9 (bottom), 60, Michael Kehoe; p. 13, Clark Quinn; p. 14, Apple Computer Inc.; p. 16 (right), Layne Kennedy; pp. 16 (bottom), 26 (bottom), 49, 50, Karen Smyth; pp. 29, 42, Travcoa Corporation; p. 56, Heidelberg USA. Jacket photo by Verne St. Clair.

The author wishes to thank the following people and organizations: Rosemary Watson, English and journalism instructor, and Patricia Garrity, Media Specialist, Somerville High School, Somerville, Massachusetts; Somerville High School students Kristen Celeste, Sandra Clifford, Van Huynh, Susue Invencio, Irvelt Jean Perrin, Nancy Soares, Bill Torres, Kris Walsh, and Dawn Wells; Verne St. Clair; Karen Smyth; Tena Robinson; the Hewlett-Packard Corporation; Steve Ivy; the desktop publishing students at Radcliffe College; Margaret Goldstein; Zach Marell; and my parents Sam and Josephine Madama for their lifelong support and encouragement.